Guatemala
Our Man in Central America

Stephen Platt

www.leveretpublishing.com

Guatemala: Our man in Central America
First published - April 2013
Second Edition - September 2017
Published by
Leveret Publishing
56 Covent Garden, Cambridge, CB1 2HR, UK

ISBN 978-1-9124600-7-6

© Stephen Platt 2017

All rights reserved. No part of this publication may be reproduced, stored in a retrieval system or transmitted in any form by any means, electronic, mechanical, photocopying, recording or otherwise, except brief extracts for the purpose of review, without the written permission of the publisher.

Guatemala
Our Man in Central America

Guatemala 2004

We stayed near Lago Amatilan and travelled around the area by bus to Antigua and Chichicastenango, and caught a flight to Tikal.

Guatemala City

2/2/04 Monday
We are at Miami airport. Our line is for Cancun, Bogota, Maracaibo and Guatemala. It takes forever. Finally a granny speaking Spanish shepherds us forward to a slow immigration officer called Garcia who is surprisingly nice and pronounces Scharlie's name without a hiccup. Once through we ring David to tell him we are on the way.

Quiene es?
David Nott, por favor?
Un momento. A pause.
Hello, who is it?
Steve.
Steve where are you?
Miami. We'll be an hour or so late.
OK. I'll be at the airport.
David sounds frail. I wonder how he is.

At first we'd been doubtful about coming. We'd met David's daughter Millie and his ex-wife Mariella at Christmas and they'd encouraged us to come. Millie and Julio have moved to Cambridge because they found life in Venezuela intolerable. They have four daughters and every time they went out of the house they felt they risked getting kidnapped.

We first met in 1970 or 71 at the cinema in Chacaito. I'd got a job in Caracas with the Ministry of Public Works. Jon was four and Frances was two. I'd been keen to find someone to climb with and had a letter of introduction to Charles Brewer who was making a name for himself as an explorer.

I went to see Charles at his home. I didn't get beyond the hallway where he showed me a large oil painting of his great-grandfather who had been the English Consul in La Guiara. Charles had the same eyes and droopy handle bar moustache. He said he was too busy to go climbing but gave me David's name and we became friends. But thirty years is a long time.

Finally we board and we watch our fellow passengers stuffing improbably large cases into the overhead lockers. A huge black stewardess with pink talons brings us coffee. Having been a dreading the journey we're glad to be on our

Scharlie, early morning at Tomi and David's home, overlooking Lake Amatitlan

way. Inside a thin metal can, buffeted by turbulence, the screens tell us the outside temperature is -75°F and our altitude is 10,688 metres.

We reach Guatemala City about 10pm, nearly 24 hours after leaving home. David is waiting at the barrier and he and Steve recognise each other without any hesitation and greet each other as if they parted only yesterday. Half-an-hour's drive through the night to Villa Nueva and we arrive at a cool dark timbered house with shining tile floors. We're sick with fatigue and car fumes but the house is calm and tranquil.

Are you hungry, asks David. No? Then just a drink and bed.

We meet Tomi, David's wife. The girls have gone to bed. Estas muy cansada, she says.

She seems reserved and quietly confident. She serves tea and we sit round the dinner table for a few minutes getting used to each other before fatigue overcomes us and we go to bed. We have a wide bed on the ground floor. We close the Venetian blinds but can hear tree frogs and a dog lapping water. Sleep!

Amatitlan

3/2/04 Tuesday

At first it looks as if the weather's bad, the light is so watery and grey. It's early, before six. Outside there is a high whistling sound followed by click clacking. Parting the blinds we can see Lake Amatitlan shrouded in mist and surrounded by purple grey mountains. The noise is from a flock of blue jays scolding in the trees around a clipped lawn. Their wings are peacock blue and flash against the vivid pink of the bougainvillaea. Two large pine trees catch the wind making them sigh and sing. The sun comes up over the mountains and the world changes from monochrome to colour.

Coming upstairs for breakfast we see the lake through the French doors. Misty and mysterious, it fills our view with reflections from the surrounding hills. To the far right is Pacaya with its perfect conical shape and plume of smoke. David is excited as he talks about the wonderful colours when it erupts. Lago Amatitlan is polluted. Untreated chemical effluent from factories goes straight into the river that feeds the lake.

Fish still survive but I don't know if they're safe to eat, says David.

David is gentle with grey hair, thick glasses and a crumpled face. His voice is quiet and calm and he seems happy in this house surrounded by women. Tomi comes from a large family in the eastern part of the country and as well as

David's family – Jenny , Tomi, David, Carina, Luqui and Dora – in their garden

their own two daughter they have three other young relative living with them. They have been up since five getting the girls out of the house.

We meet Jenny, the eight-year-old, dressed in a brown school uniform. She's waiting for her lift to school. We meet Carina, the eldest, who is twenty. She's working as a dental supplies sales rep. to pay her way through a college course in personnel management. Luqui, in her first year as a primary school teacher, has already left for work. We meet Dora and Luis. Dora helps lay the table and Luis is pottering in the garden. The house seems like a little business enterprise.

On the balcony David explains the view. A half-finished building to our left is a church. Reinforcing bars protrude from bare concrete. The church will have a domed roof.

Originally there was going to be a minaret, says David.

Madre Innes, daughter of one of the fourteen great families in Guatemala, has joined an Anchorite order of nuns. She works with destitute children and is building a church in front of David's house. David says Madre Innes is young, beautiful and charming. She's also ruthless and very determined. David knows he's lost the battle but has convinced himself that it could have been much worse. Softened by tall trees the church will frame his view.

Next door the neighbours have started a business grinding tree roots to make herbal medicine for diabetics. The idea is to retrieve the failing fortunes of their photographic business.

The water is shut off because the electricity bill hasn't been paid. All this is destroying the tranquillity of David's life. Tomi is worried about the stress it causes him. They have been here fifteen years and David is settled here.

We have coffee and David shows Scharlie his garden. It's the start of the dry season many shrubs and trees have come into flower. There is a deep blue jacaranda, a truly tropical tree, but because we're in the highlands and it is relatively cool, there is almond and peach blossom. There are avocado trees weighed down with fruit and oranges and bananas. A profusion of things sold as houseplants in England carpet the grounds – tradescantia and begonias, philodendron and amaryllis with their huge scarlet trumpets. A pawpaw tree stands straight and proud with its umbrella leaves and its spiral of fruit, green turning to half-ripe yellow.

We sit to eat – a substantial meal of ham omelettes with roast potatoes, tortillas and frijoles. Scharlie asks how the beans are cooked. There are frijoles parados, or whole beans, and frijoles pureed.

Tomi asked if we like them because, she says with a laugh, we will be eating a lot of them during our stay.

David says he's never got used to tortillas and that's why he makes his own sourdough bread.

Although it is cloudy and stormy looking, it will not rain till May. We wait for the house to dry out and then we do the repairs, says David.

We decide to accompany David to Villa Nueva to go to the bank and pay his dues for the water supply which is shared with the local village. No hot water. It's politics, says David.

We get in the car and drive to the village on the hill. We stop at the community office, a single storey concrete block painted with political slogans. There is a meeting already in progress. We are offered seats and a man explains that they are discussing the problem David has come about – the water. Another man takes over and explains that the electricity company has cut off the supply because their bill hasn't been paid for a year. He says that the committee are asking each neighbour for a contribution.

How much, asks David.

Six hundred Quetzales, the man says.

David says that's a lot and a woman sitting against the wall agrees.

The atmosphere is friendly and constructive. Various solutions are being considered including returning to the original company that used to supply the water. David tells us the community lobbied the municipality to take over the water supply from the company because they said they charged too much. The spokesman says they had assumed they would save money but now it's costing more and the supply is unreliable.

David says that we are visitors from England and that we need to wash. The man says then perhaps we can help by chipping in. They all laugh.

We find out where we have to pay. A man who hasn't spoken yet says that they plan to replace the three pumps with a one small unit to the save electricity. The spokesman wants to show us a catalogue but David just wants to get on.

At the bank in Villa Nueva the queue snakes round in a long line and David decides to come back another time. Villa Nueva he says is reputed to have more girlie bars than churches. The centre of the town has been paved and landscaped.

How long has it been like this? asks Scharlie.

It was done recently, because there was an election. They lost, David says, smiling. The new government is supposed to be less corrupt – we'll see. More than half the population is Mayan but the whites have everything.

How did you come to be in Guatemala? asks Scharlie.

Because of Belize, David says. I came in 1969 when Guatemala was making noises about invading. I was trying to find out how imminent it was.

It seems such an odd thing to say that we ask who sent him.

He hesitates. It's twelve years since I finished so it shouldn't matter to tell you. I wasn't a journalist, I was working for MI6.

We're stunned. It seems such a bizarre idea, this quiet gentle man a spy. So we just look at each other and say nothing.

We go to the shopping mall to buy a newspaper – David wants to check on jobs for Luis. We also stop at the plumbers' supplies and find out that he has overscrewed the stopcock in the road. It upsets him and makes him abstracted.

Later at home Tomi says, it's stress. She gives him a massage – chopping his neck helps, she says. She is quite robust, saying it couldn't be fatal as he's she's done it for 20 years and he's still here. She describes how he sometimes cries out with frustration.

I could cure it with three shots of rum, says David. I used to struggle to a bar and with each drink I'd feel better. But I'm an alcoholic so drink's no remedy.

This is David's third family. It's the only one I've been able to stay with long enough to see them grow up, he says.

He must have been in his fifties when he met Tomi. She was nineteen, he says. We were both at low ebb and decided to join forces for a while.

He helps Jenny with her homework and encourages her English. He's proud of both his daughters but is concerned about their future.

When I pop off, he says, I'd like to know they are alright.

Scharlie goes off for a sleep. Time doesn't seem to matter and her big breakfast means she's not hungry. She sleeps until four. After a cup of rosella tea we go for a walk with David and Jenny down to the lake. The narrow track has been widened with a big earth-mover. Madre Innes has bought a plot on a promontory with fantastic views. David is concerned by what she's planning to do here. The banker who owned all this area has lost interest in development and has given her the land. She's going to build a dormitory for homeless boys and a chicken farm for them to work in. The other residents are not pleased, but say they can do nothing. Her family is well connected. Part of the building boom is due to rival evangelical churches outdoing each other in the size of their churches.

Jenny picks up pebbles that catch her eye. She finds a piece of obsidian, and pops itinto her shirt pocket. She has a collection of stones. More and more I think she is like Jessica, our grand-daughter.

We reach the lake after a twenty-minute walk and see a substantial mansion. The lawns and gardens are beautifully groomed and there is a jetty and a boat. It's such a surprise after the wild bush we have been walking through.

It's a weekend house, David says. The owners used to come with motorbikes, motorboats, and water-skis.

It's hard to imagine dancing and carousing in this quiet dignified place.

The old man got killed trying to keep up with his sons on a motorbike and they haven't been back since, says David.

So many stories of fortunes made and squandered or squittered away as David would say. Sons inheriting great wealth then sinking into apathy and inaction.

We sit on a fallen log by the water's edge. David comments on its rough surface and how it used to be smooth. We watch Jenny peeling off chunks of bark and toss them in the lake. No wonder the trunk is rough.

The water hyacinth growing on the margin is a problem. It forms floating islands that we can see in the distance and blocks the outflow of the lake where there is a hydro-electric plant.

There are vegetated cliffs behind us. The rock looks compact and holdless. David bemoans the loss of his climbing equipment and the passage of time.

There is a much bigger cliff near where we used to live and a guiding company introduces beginners to climbing by dragging them up difficult climbs, he says.

Back home Tomi cooks rice and chicken flavoured with honey and callaloo, the local spinach. In spite of our rest we're tired and in bed by nine.

Antigua

Wednesday 8/2/04

Over breakfast we talk about attempts to grow vegetables and their lack of success with carrots and parsnips. Their chickens have been eaten. The dog took a dozen and a fierce rodent, called at tacquazin, another twelve. Tomi said it isn't worth trying to be self-sufficient; fruit and veg are cheap in Guatemala.

David and Tomi are taking us to Antigua today. It's a forty-minute hairpin drive over a mountain range into another valley.

Antigua is a beautiful old town with wide cobbled streets on a strict north-south, east-west grid. Once the capital, there are streets and streets of stately Spanish colonial houses with long deep corridors of rooms leading off each other. Light comes from an inner courtyard. These patios are lushly planted, dust-free and cool. In the last few years the houses have been bought by the middle classes and prices have risen. Although David loves his house overlooking the lake he feels it might be have been better for Tomi and the girls if they had bought a house here 15 years ago when property was cheap.

We wander about in a leisurely way, popping into galleries and shops. We buy postcards, trying to find some of Pacaya erupting at night to send the grandchildren. Several houses are being used as art galleries. The paintings are in bright bold colours. Tomi has been painting for several years, developing an individual abstract style after being introduced to finger painting by her stepson,

Antigua. Founded in 1543 and once the capital of Guatemala, it was destroyed by earthquakes in 1717 and 1773 and is now a UNESCO World Heritage Site.

David. She would love to make a business and sell her paintings.

I haven't done any for a while, she says. When I was painting it took over everything. You have to paint until you finish. If you let the paint dry it's very difficult. But the girls didn't like me being so preoccupied.

Tomi takes Scharlie into the covered market. You only have to glance sidelong at an item for the vendor to come forward. Being with Tomi helps. She's fierce at bargaining and has some idea what the price should be. Your senses are assailed by colour and you think who can I buy this for? Scharlie buys two bead bracelets and a quartz pendant. Steve is collared by a saleswoman who offers him hand-embroidered wall-hangings for a dollar. She's very persistent but the price seems crazy and he feels confused and tries not to encourage her.

We go in search of food and wander through the main square to a delightful restaurant serving a choice of meat dishes and a variety of salads for a fixed price of 35 Quetzales or about $4. Four steel pots contain stew – chicken, pork, beef or a mixture. There are lots of vegetables and salads to choose from. We point to the dishes we want and then walk through with our plates to the

Ruins of Iglesia del Carmen, Antigua

Scharlie has a soft spot for parrots

patio in the back. Scharlie falls for the green parrots on a perch. One jumps to the floor and she persuades the waiter to let her put it on her shoulder. She looks like long John Silver.

Tomi shows us a copy of the Revue, the English language magazine. The front cover is a photo of an old man, white haired and bewhiskered. He's sitting on a park bench, immaculate in dark suit, white shirt, tie and Homburg hat. He holds a cane, eyes alert to the retreating form of a short skirt and slender legs that are disappearing out of the picture.

Don David, we say.

Viejo verde, laughs Tomi and smacks him affectionately.

After lunch we pass a tourist agency and we go in make bookings for Lago Atitlan and Tikal. Atitlan is surrounded by steep volcanoes and is much larger than David's lake, Amatitlan. Later, at home, in the evening, David notes all times we need delivering and collecting and makes sure we had an alarm clock.

Back home we settle down to write the postcards we've bought. David says the postal system here has only recently emerged from chaos. He went a year without bank statements as any letter that looked as if it might contain money was opened and then thrown away. There were numerous Express postal agencies all as bad as each other. Recently the government contracted a Canadian agency to sort it out and now the mail works. There are no postboxes so we try to write all our cards before going on an expedition to the post office in Villa Nueva.

Tomi makes us feel welcome and looked after. She has a strong light body and stands like a tree planted firmly. Her humour is quick and her dark eyes gleam as she smiles and gives a throaty laugh. David obviously relies on her for the practical round of daily living. He often touches her gently with a little pat, partly like a child wanting comfort, partly a father giving a benediction. She has a routine of doing the housework everyday before other business or pleasure. The shining tiles are washed down and polished with a sweeping motion of a cloth on the end of a broom. She has an easy manner with us and talks in Spanish but understands if we answer in English. She is quiet and none directive with her children but when she calls, Jenny responds at once.

David is hard to describe. One's first impression is of a gentle old man with thick glasses, grey hair and precise, almost fastidious, movements. He has quiet, slightly slurred, speech and he often illustrates his points with physical movements like a squirrel eating a nut. Instead of words he often uses little mimicking pantomimes that are funny and to the point. He stands erect in his slippers, shoulders back and hands clasped like a ballet dancer over his stomach. His eyes crease with fun and mischief. When he let drop that he had been an MI6 agent for over thirty years it was at both ridiculous and entirely believable. Now at 75 years his eye for detail and his ability to savour life is still giving him an energy which is infectious.

Steve made tea and we sit at the dinner table with Tomi. David talks about Fawcett, his publisher in New York, who has a ski lodge in Vermont. They used to go but David thinks it is too extravagant and can't see the point. Maybe he won't travel again. He's obviously done his share. But it would be nice to get him over to England. He might want to visit Millie.

One can see in his painting that he feels nostalgic about England. And often talks about his youth climbing in North Wales when he did two hard climbs, Bellevue Bastion and Lots Groove, at the age of seventeen.

I last saw him in Cambridge in 1976 with Mariella, Milly and his son David. He'd just spent a glorious weekend in Llanberis when he did Great Wall with Jim Perrin. For a while great Wall had been the hardest climb in Wales. David shows us a photograph taken by Pete Crew. He looks composed on the improbably steep wall. He recounts how, in the Padarn Lake Hotel, Joe Brown, the all time great of British climbing, had asked him what he'd done that day. Great Wall, said David proudly. After a pause Brown says, only doing one a day then.

Thursday 9/2/04
We wake an hour or so before the alarm, which had been set for five, and are ready to leave before six. David wants to beat the traffic and get to Antigua early.

For 40 years I've pondered what is wrong with this place, says David.

Guatemala? we ask.

No, Latin-America, the whole lot. Maybe it's a defective gene. It's the Spanish character, Cervantes wrote about it. The Hidalgo with a toothpick in his hat as if he's had a good lunch, when in fact he's starving. Pride and honour first. You, yourself. Then family; maybe one's extended family. Never society or your fellow man. I can't abide the arrogance, the idleness of the elite, the wastrel landowner with thousands of acres.

If you mess up the system as much as Latin America it's no wonder people behave irresponsibly. We act selflessly if it makes sense. Here there's no point. The police and the politicians are all corrupt. If your neighbour thinks you're foolish for acting correctly, if people admire the slick dodge, then that's what you get, says Steve.

Some words are black – honour, righteousness, says David.

What about virtue? askes Steve.

Like the Roman idea of virtu? Duty, steadfastness, courage – they're good. We need virtue.

What proportion of population is Maya?

Over half. Two per cent are white and they have everything. And the rest, are mixed, ladino or mestizo. Commentators suggest we're all ladino now. But that's not true. The majority are pure Maya, and they have nothing. But they're getting organised. There are people helping them, showing them what to do, what to demand. Three thousand years of culture and still going strong.

This division is what's wrong with this country, says David. I can't stand the rich Criollo – their arrogance, their lack of sympathy, their racial intolerance.

I had a boat, a thirty footer, he says. I was in Kingston, Jamaica. But you can't live on a boat in the tropics, it's too hot. It was when Manley was President and we were worried about the place going red. I knew an old couple from Carolina who lived on a yacht in the marina. She was a delightful white-haired biddy shelling peas or knitting all the time. We were talking about Michael Manley. That red, that commie bastard, says David, imitating her Southern drawl and spitting out the words. He wants stringing up, the nigger, wants doing for, like that Luther King.

It's chilly standing outside the agency waiting for the bus and we regret not bringing something warm to wear. The driver is late.

It's now we worry that we're waiting in the wrong place, says David.

We talk about anything and everything, trying to catch up on the past.

Do you like living in the tropics? we ask. No, the immediate reply. So where would you like to live in England? I don't know, anywhere, he said, as though it was once relevant, but is no longer.

Would Carina come back here if she went to England to study? Probably not. Why? Too circumscribed, too limiting, he says.

We are still shivering on the corner outside Sinfronteras offices and decide to wander down to the square. We find a cafe and order cafe con leche, milky coffee, and biscottis.

That old flame I told you about yesterday, says David, the American who looked me up a couple of years ago, the one I got into trouble about with Tomi. She took me to task for a living out in Amatitlan. She said Antigua would be much better for the girls. It wasn't right that they were locked up out in the sticks.

But you love it there, says Scharlie. It's peaceful and beautiful. You could move here now, if you wanted to, says Steve. It's never too late. Yet it is, says David.

You and Tomi seem very happy, says Scharlie. Yes it's a good match we complement each other.

What are you doing today, we ask. Fix the water; order a water truck, says David. And the man who came last night? Rene, the nephew of my neighbour Alberto, David says. They have a small tank and he wants to share the water delivery. There was a scare a while ago and Alberto offered to lend me a shotgun. I had my pistol, but the shotgun's better. It was a beautiful object, one of the most exquisite things I've ever seen. Made in London.

One of the nuns telephoned and said there were men with guns in the convent and would I go and help. Once I got there the nuns had got one of the men tied with wire and were grilling him. They were resolute and tough. Where are the others,? How many of you? There's one with a rifle, said Madre Carmen. She asked me to go and find him. I thought, you don't go after a man with a rifle if you've only got a pistol. I said we should wait for the police. The police arrived and took one look. They said nothing, just freed his hands of the wire and led him off for a pee. He had been on a floor for hours.

Hard to imagine this Pickwickian character, as our man in the Caribbean. A real-life James Bond; blinking over the top of his glasses. Solicitous of our creature comforts; gentle and loving with his daughters. Yesterday he rather diffidently showed us the tourist shoulder bag in which he carries his pistol. We'd been talking about climbing the volcano Pacaya that you can see from his veranda and he plans on taking the pistol for protection.

You can't draw on someone holding a gun on you, he says. When they ask for the money I just put my hand in here as if I'm getting out my wallet, raise my arm and shoot through the bag.

The bag rattles. That's the ammo, says David. It's not like the telly, not how they do it in the movies, with two hands on the gun pointing it up. You may need a hand to steady yourself if you're moving round a house. And when you bring the pistol down to fire it's in your line of sight hiding the target. No, you use one hand and always bring the pistol up from below, arms straight, both eyes open.

They trained you?

Yes, we began with all that. Weeks in what we called the fortress in a place on the coast.

Chichicastenango

The mini-bus arrives and we are on our way by seven. First stop is Chichicastenango.

In the bus we talk about the relative merits of international aid and tourism. Maybe tourism is as least as useful as aid. The countryside is orderly and tidy. The land is divided into small plots growing vegetables in strict rows. The soil looks fertile and the methods seem modern. There are trees wherever the terrain is too steep to plant. This is the start of the dry season and the landscape is still very green. Many of the trees are in blossom, putting down seed for the wet season.

Today is market day in Chichicastenango. The driver drops us at the main hotel, a beautiful old colonial building with a wide patio and fountain. We have a coffee and a rest before venturing forth. The main street slopes down gently to the church with stall after stall selling the gaudy artesania of Central America. A coral necklace catches Scharlie's eye but she says she'll look around first.

Thursday market in Chichicastenango

Copal and penitents outsdie Santo Tomas

Copal is burning in incense burners outside the church. Tourists are being taken into a side chapel to see Maximon, the cult figure we'd read about in the guide.

Wandering from the church we hear explosions and realise that they are fireworks. A procession led by musicians with flutes and skin drums is coming towards us. Four men carry a religious statue – but this doesn't look like anything Christian. The men, dressed in native costume, are followed by the women, also in traditional dress. They climb the steps to the church and kneel outside. A Criollo in a straw cowboy hat and boots pours white spirit into a glass held by one of the kneeling elders who, in turn pours, it out in a line on the stone paving.

People are taking photos and I descend the steps and wait for a moment to get a shot. One of the men, who carries a toy white horse tied with ribbons and bows, hovers in the shadows of the doorway. They move the statue round to each of the cardinal points and pour more spirit on the stones. The man with the horse comes into the open and someone hands him a wicker globe wrapped with firecrackers. He dances around with the things blasting off. One of them chars his shoulder blanket.

Steve is approached by a young girl who turns out to be the one who

K'iche Maya in traje de Maxeño letting off fireworks before the procession leaves the church

accosted him in Antigua. Three hunred mister. I saw you in Antigua, she says giggling. It han' made, says the girl. I don't want it, Steve protests. Your wife she like. For you special price, two hunred. Han' made. Sorry but I don't want it, Steve squeaks. OK for you, twenty dollar. Sorry no, says Steve. What you give me? But your wife she like. Sorry, says Steve limply. For me, the money – children, school. No, Steve says, feeling increasingly distressed.

Scharlie is way up the street negotiating for two delicate coral and amethyst bracelets and Steve has been caught by the shoeshine boy. Steve says his shoes aren't dirty, but the boy disagrees.

Venga, come on, Steve says and the boy starts on his shoes. He finishes with a flick of his rag.

Quanto? Steve asks the shoeshine boy. Diez Quetzales, he says. Esto es precio para gringos, says Steve. Sure, he agrees. Steve gives him six. The lad looks thoughtful but doesn't argue. Meanwhile Scharlie has done a deal for two coral necklaces for 20 Quetzales. We still have to run the gauntlet of the sales girl from Antigua and her friends.

For you special price, one hunred and fifty, says the girl, plonking the red weaving on Steve's folded arms.

I'm puzzled, says Steve. You offered us the same thing for a dollar in Antigua.

Para mirar, she says. A dollar to look, she says.

How hard-hearted can you get, Steve thinks, as he lets it slide off. She catches it deftly and plonks it on his shoulder again. We try and walk away.

One hunred, she says, desperation creeping into her voice.

Scharlie is at the next stall starting negotiations for a bead bag. Steve begins to crack.

I can't stand this, he says as the girl puts the mantel on his shoulder again.

Like cowards, we hurry back to the sanctuary of the hotel and its polite tranquillity. What a privileged existence we live. The vendors try to catch your eye and when you refuse they think it's because you're sticking out for a lower price. Their enterprise and persistence is admirable. The girl must have come in a truck with her friends and sisters. We wonder who organises it all and who makes all this stuff? How often does she make a sale and who profits when she does?

A waiter in full traditional dress and with the face of a polished conker greets us and ushers us to a table. We ask for agua sin gas, still water, and say we will order lunch in a bit.

Hotel for lunch in Chichicastenango

The hotel is old colonial-style with white walls, high ceilings and black beams. Archways look onto interior courtyards. The gardens are laid out in formal geometric pattern with a fountain in the centre. The planting spills over with azaleas, hydrangeas, hibiscus all underplanted with violets. Scarlet blue and yellow mackaws stand on perches each with their little umbrellas. There are also two green parrots. Parrots give me a funny feeling in my tummy, she says. I had one when I was a child in Jamaica. I'm powerfully attracted to them and want to have them sidle on to my arm and let me stroke them.

A band strikes up on the balcony above us. There is a Guatemalan xylophone, drums and a cello-like instrument. They are very good. Steve writes his journal and Scharlie begins her postcards. The buffet lunch is superb. We have a fantastic meal. For about £8 we can choose as many dishes as we want. There is a variety of salads for openers, not just greens and tomatoes, but a beautifully presented variety of rice, tuna, and many other cold dishes. We return for the second course of hot meat stews, roast potatoes, chips, roast corn and the ubiquitous frijoles and tortillas. Steve has a beer, Gallo again, that David recommended yesterday. And the waiter is back with an armful of puddings. Scharlie has a crystallised fruit, called manzanilla and Steve has fresh melon, papaya and pineapple. We decide we won't need to eat again today. Scharlie takes a photograph of the mackaws and it is time to leave to catch our bus leaves to Panajachel on Lake Atitlan.

On the bus journey everywhere looks so fertile and orderly. In the deep sided ravines the slopes are terraced, forming sharp geometric shapes ready

Lunch buffet in Chichicastenango

Scarlet macaws

for planting. In the flatter areas patches of maize stalks stand drying, waiting to be burned off. A woman bundles Arum lilies and another group of women spread newly harvested oranges out in a field.

Waiting for the bus

Panajachel and Lake Atitlan

Another two hours takes us to Panajachel. As we come down into the valley the air thickens with an oppressive grey haze. The first view of the lake is dramatic with the steep mountains diving into the water and forming a huge circle as if it had been a single gigantic volcano which had blown its top.

We enter another delightful hotel. This one is Italian-owned and built in single storey terraces with rooms opening onto verandas. There is a garden planted with palms and soft green lawns and a small pond of glittering blue water in the centre.

Until recently Lake Atitlan was undeveloped and provided a good livelihood to the Mayan villages which crowd its shores. Fish were plentiful and the menfolk built dug-out canoes from the large trees growing on the lower slopes of the volcanoes. Recently, holiday villas and hotels have been springing up and an alien fish – the black bass has beenintroduced for sport fishing. It cannot be caught in surface nets from canoes but only by divers with harpoons and it has decimated the native fish stock. It has also wiped out the local water bird by taking its young from the nests in the reed beds. Selling craft goods to tourists is now the mainstay of the economy. Each area has its own patterns and colour combinations.

We wander up and down the main street. We try, without success, to get money out of a 'hole-in-the wall' cash machine. A young American girl, who has been travelling for a month and thinks Guatemala is 'awesome', says that only one in four machines work. There is quite a small crowd watching, as if waiting for a miracle.

We'd spotted a rug as we got out of a bus and had, without trying, bargained the woman down to 125 Quetzales, or about £18. The rug is 8 ft square in beige, green and dark blue and we wonder if it would fit at Leveret Croft. In the kitchen the wool would absorb too much grease. Maybe it isn't quite the right size and shape. These decisions take energy – shopping is not our forte. We decided to get it for the 'one day to be finished' barn back home. But the cash machine doesn't work and we decide we need to husband our money for the trip.

We wander down to the lake three or four minutes away, passing more stalls of colourful clothes and rugs. There is a sandy beach and a promenade spilling

over with bougainvillaea and jacaranda. We stop at a beach-side shack with faded pink tablecloths and duck egg blue tables. The colours look wonderful in the evening light and we watch the sun setting over the lake while the proprietor and her granddaughter prepare tea for us. Scharlie has really taken to black tea without any sugar.

We go back to the hotel for a shower. Warm water is welcome after the last few days washing with a jug of cold-water. Sitting in bed we work through the postcards, deciding which to send to whom. There is one with a macaw like we saw at lunch-time in Chichicastenango. The caption reads: Guacamaya or scarlet macaw. For years it was usual to see these beautiful birds flying in pairs over the crowns of trees. Now they are fast on the way to extinction.

Awake last night, unable to sleep with the sound of dogs and the snoring of our next-door neighbour, I thought about a conversation and tried to fix it in my mind.

From time to time David has let slip snippets of his life as an intelligence officer. I was studying a map in the corridor outside the bedroom at David's. It was undated but clearly old. It mapped the routes of the Spanish galleons and where different crops and natural resources could be found. It was in English and beautifully drawn.

It was my leaving present, said David. Nicer than a Rolex. I like to think that someone at head office had an understanding. It was my patch of course. It's an original. Came out in the diplomatic bag. They got it framed beautifully.

I had to drive to Mexico every three weeks or so to report to my control because the people in the embassy were known to both the Colonels and the guerrillas.

We are the Prozac generation. We pop a pill to cope with our problems of sleeplessness or depression. I had problems with panic attacks. I went to a doctor in London – someone the firm used. I asked what could be done. Nothing, you're burnt-out, that's all. That, and the end of the Cold War, and I was finished. No one was interested in the Caribbean any longer.

Friday   6/2/04

We wake up to sun and blue sky and have breakfast in the circular dining hut thatched with palm leaves. We choose chapin, the traditional Guatemalan breakfast the waiter recommends. It turns out to be scrambled eggs, beans and fried banana - surprise! The waiter is solicitous and grave. What must these polite people make of us gringo tourists.

After breakfast we sit and read the guide. It catalogues injustices around this lake since Pedro de Alvarado. The latest atrocities were by the army in the eighties. Finally the people of Santiago, one of the villages we will go to today, kicked the military out in 1990. Now the place is being invaded by developers and the rich.

We stop at the post office to buy stamps and leave the cards we have written so far. The minibus arrives promptly at 9.30. We've paid for everything in Antigua and show our tickets to the driver who takes us the few hundred yards to the lakeside. There are several launches at wooden jetties and we are shepherded to ours.

On the jetty a little girl offers us necklaces. Steve tries to take a picture but she ducks away, saying five Quetzales for a necklace and a photo. Steve says she's a good businesswoman and pays her. We climb aboard. The engine is idling and smelling strongly of diesel. We sit on benches under an awning and are glad when we get going and the wind blows the fumes away.

The outlines of the volcanoes surrounding the lake are pale grey in the morning mist. The sun gets higher. The day is clear and blue and the water is

Boarding the launch for the boat trip around Lake Atitlan

calm. The surface is uniformly criss-crossed by little ripples like the wrinkles on jam when it is just about to set. They refract the light and pick up a rosy pink from the mountain slopes. The colours are the pinks and greens of the cafe we sat in yesterday.

We have binoculars and study the mountains. We're surrounded by the wooded crater of an enormous extinct volcano. The cultivation of the steep ground is impressive – orderly terraces using every bit of ground. We see maize, peas, broad beans, potatoes and tomatoes. On the steeper slopes there are vertical grass banks between the terraces. It's all neat and tidy and we wondered if the people working in the fields own their land or if they are they tenants.

A girl sits next to Scharlie and asks where we come from. After a couple of pleasantries she has her wares spread out. Her mother is working on the couple opposite. She plonks a shirt on the man. It's blue, it suits him. Then she unwinds her hair and shows the woman how it is wound with a long strip of cloth and tied into a turban. The woman indicates that she has short hair. Undaunted the sales woman wraps the woman's head in a colourful scarf and puts the strip around that . It looks good. Then she turns to us and plonks a red-striped shirt on me. She has an eye for what might suit people. Scharlie's says it looks good so we buy it. Just as we're arriving at San Pedro another passenger asks if she has a blouse like the one she and her daughter are wearing. She unbundles her wares and makes another sale.

Our first stop is San Pedro. This used to be a favourite haunt of hippies. There

San Pedro, Lake Atitlan

are small houses set in gardens full of fruit and vegetables that cluster along the main street and down to the water's edge. Further inland there is a labyrinth of earth paths weaving complicated routes around garden plots. There seem to be no big developments or hotels just lots of small enterprises like Spanish language classes or horse riding.

The village is also famous for its coffee and we see conical heaps of berries being stirred in the sun by men with long shovels. Once the skins are removed the beans are laid out in the sun to dry. Apparently young gringos used to congregate here to get stoned on cocaine but finally the locals got fed up and threw them out. There are still a few young Americans but maybe they are just enjoying the cheap living and are behaving themselves.

Mother and daughter sales team on Lake Atitlan

We walk to the aguas thermales, the hot springs, but they are still filling the pools. It's all so underdeveloped and rustic. It would be nice to spend more time here but we have an hour. It's all rather rushed. We find a cafe with tables under the trees and Steve has a coffee while Scharlie orders a papaya con leche milkshake. At the table next to ours an American is having a Spanish lesson while having lunch with his teacher, a girl of twenty or so. Scharlie's relieved we can use of their primitive toilet behind a curtain before we have to head back to the jetty.

Back on the launch the wind has risen and the surface of the lake ripples like the pattern of the board Tomi uses for her paintings. To David's disapproval, she insists on painting on the rough side of the hardboard. The water is green but still reflects the pink of the hillsides and the blue of the sky. The steep slopes of the San Pedro volcano are a patchwork of tiny plots. They're growing maize, coffee and crops we can't identify despite using the binoculars. Next stop, Santiago Atitlan.

The guide waiting on the dock offers to take us to see Maximon, but we prefer to saunter. We walk up a steep hill past the usual stalls and find a market in full swing. This is a real market for locals, selling fruit, vegetables, ropes, tools, second-hand radios and music tapes.

We sit in the square and eat our packed lunches. We are the only tourists and it's interesting to see the fruit and vegetables people are buying. Small green mangoes are popular – apparently they are eaten with salt.

A gnarled Maya is loading a lorry with huge rope bags full of avocados. Two big guys have to help get the bag on to

Bagging coffee beans in San Pedro

Coffe and papaya at the Aguas Thermales

Santiago Amatitlan

his shoulders. We can hardly see him under his load. He has to cross the square and climb the steep ramp into the back of the truck. He jogs back for the next bag. They look heavy. He has a pink towel on his head that hangs down his back to protect his neck, knee-length shorts and a rope belt with a strange-looking stirrup like object. He loads a couple of dozen bags while we eat lunch.

This looks a prosperous market town. The women wear a different type of blouse to the women on the launch – white cotton with flowery embroidery. On the way back we get off the main street and thread our way through beaten earth paths leading past back doors. Scharlie says she feels nervous but there is absolutely no sense of menace and all the people we've met have

Market day in Santiago Amatitlan, and houswives buying 'spinach'

Avocado

Santiago Amatitlan

been gentle and friendly. The guidebooks keep warning of rape and robbery but maybe this is in more isolated areas.

From here we travel east. The launch hugs the coast at first as we make for our last stop, San Antonio. There are holiday homes with well-tended gardens and little jetties on the rocks with thatched huts for picnic places. Scharlie is beginning to feel a bit sick with the vibration from the boat and the sun.

We get off and wander up towards the village. Women are sitting on the beach sorting onions. Tomi says later that they sell them for barbecues. They pick them when they are still young, with the leaves and stalk. Steve snatches a photograph. One of the women looks aggrieved and tells her toddler to hide. Perhaps the idea that children's souls can be stolen by a photograph is not so

Chichicastenango market

Santiago market

Women sorting onions in San Antonio   *Climbing up into the village*

far-fetched. After all the Maya used to use children for sacrifice. As recently as a couple of years ago a Japanese tourist was murdered by villagers in Todos Santos de Cuchumatanes for taking photographs of children.

San Antonio is a working village and hasn't been tarted up for tourists. The steep track is dusty and small concrete houses rise in tiers. Maize and coffee are spread to dry on the flat roofs. Chickens move stiff-legged in the drains beside the path. It's dusty and hot.

We watch a man weaving cloth on a loom and two women hand-weaving. We go into a house where a man is spinning red yarn. He greets us courteously but doesn't stop. It's not clear whether we have just wandered into somebody's private dwelling.

We are feeling tired but we walk along the hillside observing life. Further along the winding path a couple of carpenters are making a new loom out of pine. One is planing what looks like the treadle arm. Steve gets into conversation with him. The man says it will take them 15 days to make the loom and they will charge 2,800 Quetzales which is about £230. It's good to have any ordinary conversation and to get away from the buying and selling but it's time to go and we have to hurry back to the launch.

The afternoon haze has come down and Scharlie snoozes as we chug along. There are a lot of large villas along this part of the coast. The area seems in the throes of change.

Back at the hotel we have about half an hour to wait before our mini-bus is due. We avoid looking across the street to the rug stall and the two ladies who

Hand weaving at his loom, San Antonio   *Preparing the warp yarns*

nearly sold us a rug yesterday.

The bus back to Antigua is full and Steve gets a seat at the back next to an American couple. The man's grey hair is pulled back in a pigtail under a baseball cap. Scharlie strikes up a conversation with the young man sitting next to her. He's a tall blonde German who has been travelling for two months. He's going to Costa Rica and has learned enough Spanish to get around. He is easy to talk to and Scharlie tells him about walking in Corsica and Scotland.

Where've you been? asks the American.

We tell him.

That's really moving, he says. I hope you can remember some of it.

What are you doing here? we ask.

We run a micro bank.

What's that?

We lend small amounts of money to local people. We started five years ago in Panajachel and have spread out into the surrounding area. We employ 30 people and have about 2,700 borrowers on the books.

If you don't mind me asking, how much interest do you charge? asks Steve

Twenty percent, he says, looking slightly sheepish.

That's much higher than back home, Steve says. It must be a good business. How many defaulters have you?

Very few. We lend only to women. The average loan is $100 but we will lend up to $200 if the person has a good track record. The point is that these people cannot get a loan from a bank. They have no assets and no title to their

The bus back to David's

land. Anyway bank interest is 21%.

Are you registered as a charity? Steve asks. This obviously has a different connotation in the States because he bridles.

We are registered as a development organisation and are tax exempt, he says.

Have you read Hernando de Soto? He's a Peruvian who argues that the lack of title to land is one of the biggest brakes on development in Latin America.

I was a doctor before I retired. I was a surgeon in Vietnam. I've seen what war can do. I don't understand why the American administration doesn't learn the lessons.

I met an English Major General called Jonathan Bailey at a development conference. We were paired in a workshop. The general's job was to look into weapons systems for the British army. He talked about precision-guided weaponry and surgical strikes. Because of my pigtail he branded me as a lefty and a pacifist. He was astonished to discover that I had been in Vietnam as a surgeon with 101st Airborne.

But you were a warrior, the general said.

Sure and I saw what war does.

We get on to the subject of the Tell me about your election process? he asks.

Well it's a lot shorter than yours and we spend less than you do.

That's the most corrupting part of our system. Power is passing from national governments to big corporations that are acting irresponsibly. I read somewhere that corporations should have, in their articles of association, a responsibility for education and health in the communities and societies they operate in.

I'm incensed by how GM has been introduced throughout North America without any public debate, he says. There is no obligation to label products. America is dumping pesticides that have been banned in the States. So the fresh Guatemalan produce we buy in the States may have been contaminated by pesticides we supplied.

I'm worried about CAFTA, the Central American Free Trade Association, he says. It's a stitch-up by the developed nations to exploit forestry, mineral and cheap labour of Central America. People like the Maya will be forced off their land to live in shanty towns and countries will be raped to provide the raw materials we need in the West.

Steve is beginning to feel sick from this battering to his social conscience and the exhaust fumes in the queue down the hill into Antigua.

Have you an email, Steve asks.

He gets out his card. His name is Theodore Nigh.

David collects us in Antigua. He's been waiting for us and has had to drive round the block several times as there was nowhere to park. We have a coffee before setting off home and Steve recounts Ted's Nigh's theories about CAFTA.

He must be a real green. CAFTA, is a perfectly respectable free trade association, says David.

As we head into the country the biggest moon you've ever seen pops up over the trees.

Tomi has cooked a meal and the whole family has waited for us. The food makes us feel better immediately. We have been dying of hunger – we have only had half a sandwich and a banana since breakfast. Steve has a beer and starts telling stories about Ben and John, the merry men who work in Scharlie's garden design business.

We ask David about land registration and Ted Nigh's worries about people being forced off their land.

Tomi tried to register her house some years ago, says David. She got a lawyer to produce a paper. The woman in the Registry took one look at it and said that's worthless and threw it on the floor. That's how it is here. No one where she lives has a title to their property. But she won't get thrown off, they'd have to throw everyone off.

Amatitlan

Saturday   7/2/04

We sit on the veranda and contemplate the day. It's a sunny day with a strong breeze. The lake shimmers with reflected sunlight. There are patches of water hyacinth which clog the shoreline then break away and blow into the centre like floating green islands. Tongues of land reach almost all the way across. David says these had been formed by a build-up of silt from the river. The land is fertile and intensively farmed.

It's to be a rest day with the family. Being with them is the main point of the trip. We have lovely breakfasts of beans and maize, pasties boiled in banana leaves, tomatoes, cheese and eggs. Tomi rings the changes. Later she makes a drink of papaya and yoghurt or refreshing tamarind.

We sit around the table chatting, David reminiscing about the firm. Carina arrives and says she'd got a fine of 100 Quetzales for using her phone in the car. We talked about regulations in England and driving here.

People buy their licence for 500 Quetzales, says David.

I bought mine, says Carina, laughing. When I went to Caracas I could hardly drive because they wouldn't lend me the car and then Millie just gave me the keys and let me get on with it in Caracas. What a headache!

Talking about driving has sparked off David's memories of travelling backwards and forwards through Central America with Tomi and Carina.

David's view of Lake Amatitlan

British passport, Guatemalan wife, car with Panamanian papers, he says. It was a nightmare crossing borders. In Costa Rica we were sent back because we didn't have an exit visa.

The Firm's ruthless. Just a suggestion, they'd say. Why don't you take the wife and kid? They figured taking them with me would fuzz the suspicions of the local gendarmes. They knew the risks of travelling around Nicaragua, Salvador and Honduras with no cover.

Why didn't you tell them to go to hell?

I knew how to get around. I knew how to make it work. And then the Cousins said the Reds were hitting the islands. Why don't you swing around and see what's what. In other words get off your ass and get on down there.

Whitey arriving in the islands – dropping into a tiny black world with no cover. What did they know, what did they care? A little twin-engine plane drops into a small airstrip. I'm the only one to get off. People sitting around on oil drums thinking who's this? Businessman, tourist, spy? Have to go into the bars and buy a crate of beer for the boys. Act the fool if I had to. And there'd be some hard-eyed bloke in the corner taking it all in. I get back and report negative. They didn't like that. Didn't want to think there was nothing doing.

Then a month or two later the Cousins report Reds or Cubans in one Island or another and I'd have to go back to the same haunts. People say, your back! Same lame story – looking for a girl or whatever. Of course they were right in Grenada, but that was after my time.

In Jamaica I had to get alongside Estrada. You can imagine the flap – Moscow trained Cuban Commie in Kingston. He had been sent to start a revolution. He could have kept them flapping for ages. But he said there was no chance in Jamaica, it would take 15 years. He blew it – he said that in Jamaica communism was a non-starter. That went straight to Number 10, says David, proudly.

In Venezuela there was a time when they were interested in industrial espionage and I had to go to Maracaibo. After a few drinks I was shown the five-year plan. Thirteen volumes and me with a sheet of paper and no camera. Not exactly James Bond! There I was ransacking it all: plans for oil, steel, coal. But they didn't make use of it. And the Venezuelans didn't do it, just bits-and-pieces, a blast furnace in Zulia, whatever.

I was in a bar one night with my Commie opposite number, a Politburo type, and the gendarmes arrived. Guys in uniform around the walls. Room no bigger than this. And then the guys in civvies, much worse, checking people's identity cards. My mate goes white and cracks. He holds up his arm saying I gotta cedula. I have to drag his arm down and tell him to just drink. His cedula is a phoney. But we get away with it. So relieved we went on drinking. Occupational hazard and me a semi- alcoholic. Maybe that was the night I lost the car and came round to see you in the middle of the night.

Steve and David go off to the supermarket. They take a five-gallon bottle of water to the neighbours who have blocked loos and then drop Luis at the bus-stop. He's starting school today – classes for adults. He's just 18. He's Luqui's half-brother, that's why they look so alike.

There's a queue for the cash machine in the mall and miracle of miracles, it disgorges 1,000 Quetzales. We hang around and have a coffee, chewing the fat, talking about the ways of the world and the evils of the easy credit.

A helicopter goes over and Steve asks if it's the police.

No private, says David. There are more private helicopters here tham in Venezuela and Colombia put together, he says. Coffee barons mostly. I had a friend, someone from one of the big families. He had one to get back and forth to his haciendas. Unfortunately he ploughed in.

He tried to marry me off when I first came here. I had $200,000 so I said she needed that much herself not to feel dependent. Is that all, the friend said. I was introduced to one, fortyish, trim. I was talking to her, getting on alright, when this young ox of a lad runs up, about 19 years old, fat and red-faced, yelling Mammy. That did it.

Over lunch we talk about the roof. It leaked or it used to leak, like all the other houses in the small development. The roof is made of Roman tiles over zinc sheets laid on top of pine boards which create the ceiling above the rafters.

The roof leaks where nails had been driven through the zinc, says David. The earthquake tremors enlarge the nail holes. We had men in to fix it without much success so we decided to have a go ourselves. We had to lift and stack the tiles as we went. They're really heavy. We put on our old clothes. We got quite adept relaying the tiles, whacking in the cement every other row and smoothing it out with a trowel.

Our neighbours looked the other way when they went past. Too much to think about, says David, putting his fingers to his forehead in a characteristic gesture.

He is worried that they sleep under the concrete slab of the first floor. The house is built on a slope, so is one storey on the road and two-storeys on the garden side.

Sometimes there are tremors for a month and we sleep in the garden, says Tomi. Sometimes we've had to run-out in the middle of the night.

I wonder whether it might be better going the other way into the hall, there's less to fall on us that way, suggests David.

When there's a big tremor you can't get out of bed, says Tomi. Everything's rocking so violently you just can't move.

Do you have house insurance? we ask.

It's very expensive, so we stopped paying this year. Anyway, says Tomi, we will all be dead in our beds so it won't matter.

After lunch we go to the golf club, next door, to have a walk and a shower. The greens are immaculate and there are panoramic views of the lake and the mountains. We stroll under the pines between the fairways leaving Jenny and Dora swimming in the pool.

It's warm and sunny but there's a strong north wind and Tomi and Dora complain of the cold. We think it's marvellous. The water is still off at home so we plan to have hot showers. Perhaps because of what David has told us, there is an air of privilege about the place, which is slightly disconcerting. Tomi has put on a dress to come here and sticks close to her husband. David's chief concern is to leave his family well provided for.

If I can just last another ten years till I'm eighty-five the children should be well launched in good jobs, he says. If I can see them well settled I can depart in peace.

David joined the club for the girls. I hoped they would meet people, he says. Hoped they might find an eligible boyfriend. But they won't co-operate! There's no social life, just golf. I thought they could put on some of those tiny shorts and pretty soon a young blood would turn up. But they're not interested. They think it's boring.

I bought a share. I hope it will pay off one day. There are 450 members. The site the club owns is much bigger than the golf course and they were hoping to sell plots for expensive housing, but to date only a couple have been built. One problem is the shanty town that has grown up on the other side of the valley. The new fashionable area is to the east but the lake and the view are fabulous and it's near the capital, so it must be worth something one day.

We are trying to decide who should have the shampoo we've brought.

You don't need shampoo, says David. It's only expensive liquid soap.

The golf club

Rubbish, says Steve. You'll see the difference.

The men's locker room is on the other side of the complex from the pool and play area. You can see the thinking behind the layout.

Sometimes there are as many as 500 cars parked outside and not half that many people on the course. They're in the bar or wherever, says David.

But today, perhaps because of the wind or because it's late, there's hardly anyone about. The people playing are mainly Korean and are taking it seriously.

In the shower we get on to the subject of Mariella. All the women I've known have been higher calibre than me. When I arrived in Mexico my control used to say you change your secretaries like I change my shirts. But I got them a passport. The girls thought if they got to Mexico they'd make it across. But I don't know, they weren't that streetwise. It's not easy.

Over supper we get out Coe's book on the Maya to show Tomi that mixing limestone with the corn when it's boiled helps release amino acids and niacin. She thought the limestone was only to help free the husk but the book says that without limestone the maize would be much less nutritious and that this was one of the key factors that allowed Mesoamerica to develop.

After dinner we talk about going dancing.

We used to go out all the time but the places we used to go have closed or changed, says Tomi. Once we had been to an embassy party and had drunk rather a lot of champagne. We went on to a bar with live music. We were dancing and were intrigued that people were clapping us. We stumbled into a dance competition but were tan boracho, too drunk, to notice. And when we got home I found my dress was torn right up the back. Tomi puts her hands over her face and throws her head back laughing dabbing tears away with a napkin.

The guerrillas in El Salvador had open offices in Mexico City. Apparently the Cubans had done a deal with the Mexicans to allow this on the promise of not infiltrating. In several visits to them they said they'd take me to a guerrilla camp. I was to go to the Camino Hotel in San Salvador, telephone my room number to them in Mexico and wait to be contacted. It was a bad time. A Dutch TV film crew had just 'disappeared' – shot on the orders of the colonels for being too sympathetic to the guerrillas. I waited a day then telephoned Mexico. My contact shouted, get out, run for your life. The man I was due to meet had been shot in the street. They said he had the number of my hotel room in his pocket, maybe even my name.

Where to go? If I went to the airport they'd get me. If I ran for the border they'd ring through and stop me. So I grabbed my bag and checked out of the Camino Real double quick. I remember people were coming to the disco, as if everything was normal. Young men and women dressed for the evening, and I'm running for my life.

Presuming lightning doesn't strike twice in the same place I went to the Hotel Alameda and took the same room as the dead Dutchmen. My room number at the Camino Real was 214. The Almeda didn't have that many. It was a pathetic plan but what else? I waited in the bar. An army patrol came in to check the register. I slipped quietly into the street. They came out behind me. I expected a rifle muzzle in the back. They didn't even look at me. They'd seen my name and did nothing. Make your mind up, Nott, I said and stayed in El Salvador probing around for ten more days. No problem.

What would have happened if you'd been caught?

Probably been shot. Some time later they came into the lobby in the Camino Real and asked for a journalist called John Sutherland. The Colonels didn't like what he'd been writing. That's me, he said. He was taken out and then disappeared. That's how it was then.

They tell you when you're being trained, and remind you many times over the years, that you'll be disowned. They can pull out your nails but if you tell them what you were doing Her Britannic Majesty's government will deny it. You are on your own – otherwise there would be a diplomatic incident.

Steve says he's seen the film Salvador. Young Freedom fighters, I bet says

David smiling. Whenever I hear that phrase I laugh. They're just the same, both sides, left and right – white middle-class, running the show, bossing the same kind of guys from the slums.

In the Sixties, Carlos Andres was Minister of the Interior in Venezuela. He used guys from the barrios, the slums. They wore leather coats and shades. You wouldn't want to fall into their hands. What else could he do. Probably just told someone to sort it out and recruit some tough people.

Sunday   8/2/04
We could go to the volcano today but it's hard to get it together. David says that he's not sure if he can make it. It's cloudy to start with but by the evening it can be completely clear so its hard to plan. It would seem prudent to attach ourselves to the back of an armed party but apparently these guided tours don't actually go up and look in the crater, so we hope David can come with us.

Steve and David take Jenny and Luqui to the cinema. They park and then find the girls hanging about because the film doesn't start for an hour. So we have a coffee and buy Jenny an ice cream. We wander about killing time and Steve gets more money out for the trip to Tikal tomorrow. Back home we decide to walk over to Amatitlan, following the dirt path to the lake. Tomi stays behind because a family have arrived for a visit. It's hot despite the wind and the volcano is clear.

Nearly into the village we pass where David and Tomi used to live. The house looks uninhabited. We look at the cliffs on the other side of the road. They are about 200 ft high and split by a crack. There is a slab capped by a slanting overhang. It looks quite good, although we can't really see what the rock is like.

David and Steve reminisce about their trip to Chamonix in 1976 and about getting benighted on the Chamois-Grepon Traverse.

What happened, asks David.

We were too slow, Steve says.

I guess so. I was always unfit on those trips. Smoking and drinking is no training.

We spent all night in the bergsrung.

No, says David. We were sitting there in the dark when a guide came past with a client and I asked if this was a way down. You were annoyed because it

The walk into Amatitlan

seemed we didn't know what we were doing.

Amatitlan is like any resort. Stalls selling drinks and food line the street and the beach under the trees. At the weekend people come out from the city and the place is buzzing with stalls and barbecues. Fried fish, roasted onions still in their stalks, like the ones we saw being sorted in San Antonio and an array of sweetmeats. It looks appetising but considering the lake is polluted we won't risk it.

There are no tourists, just ordinary people out for the day and its colourful and good-humoured. Couples are walking along the front and families are arriving in trucks. It all seems very friendly. We wander down to the pier where launches are moored. One is filling up with people. There are eight or nine rows of seats and six people abreast. There is quite a swell on the lake.

They've no life belt, says David. I don't imagine many of the passengers can swim. It's a disaster waiting to happen.

The women frying fish want us to eat, but David says that they've been using the same fat for a hundred years.

Scharlie's thirsty and keen to try a coconut. David has been looking for a saleswoman with ice but Scharlie says she prefers it without. It reminds her of home in Jamaica. We buy a fresh green coconut. The salesman deftly slices of the top with two of three strokes of his machete and hands it over with a straw. It's nectar from her childhood but there's only a little jelly when it's cut open.

We sit on the concrete seat around the tree in the centre of the town and get talking about Liverpool. David, like Steve, was brought up in Liverpool. He'd even been to the same school, Quarry Bank, before going on to the Institute. He lived near Sefton Park. We talk about St John's Market where you could buy parrots and all manner of tropical produce.

Did you go straight from Liverpool to university?

No I was in the army in Somaliland with a light infantry regiment. Once I took 300 black troops from Mogadishu to Nairobi. We had a sergeant, but I was the ranking officer, David says in his diffident way, screwing up his face.

We had to circle the lorries at night, inside an eight foot thorn fence. There was no one for miles. And a lion outside coughing in the night. Nothing like it.

You climbed Kilimanjaro.

Yes, twice. No one got leave but the general let me go. I went up quickly, in two days. On the way down I met a group that asked me to go back up with him. I had to go back down for food and then chase back after them. So I did it twice, in four days.

We debate how to get back home. David is a still a bit distracted. This morning, after a wakeful night, he has been very vague. The way he describes it is his mind is cloudy. Now we can't decide how to get back. We could go by launch, but we doubt they would land us and anyway they're all overloaded. Or we could rent a rowing boat and the boatman could row it back. But the wind's against us and it'll take forever. We could walk, but Scharlie doesn't fancy it in this heat.

How about a taxi? we ask.

Finally we run for a chicken bus and have a nice ride to Solano.

The buses are more civilised than they look from the outside. It's full and it's

Amatitlan

Green cocunut milk

stimulating to be back on a bus again. We used to travel this way in Ecuador. Because the driver stops frequently to let people on and off, the door is open and it's very airy inside.

A little girl screams and clings to her mother who tries to calm her with the breast. Perhaps she's not been on a bus before. Apart from the driver we have a huckster, who rustles up trade by shouting, 'Diez y ocho, Plaza Bolivar', at any likely-looking bystanders, and a man in a yellow football shirt with a distinguished moustache who acts as our conductor and collects the fares.

Couples with children climb aboard and single young women carrying infants in arms. Everyone looks clean and well dressed. Maybe Sunday is the day to go visiting. The buses are painted in bright colours and have massive chrome grills and a big horn on their cabin rooms. From Solano we hop on a second bus to the square in Villa Nueva. We try a taxi but they want 40 Quetzales. The buses are 1 Quetzales each. So we hop on a third bus. The driver shoots off at a great pace, overtaking a line of stalled traffic and diving into an improbably small gap to avoid the oncoming traffic. He's a killer, says David. He's one who runs off the road and kills fifteen or more of his passengers.

We get off at the mall, buy a phonecard and call home. Carina comes and collects us and takes us home to lunch – spaghetti Bolonaise, with a Guatemalan flavour, and fresh melon. Everyone is in a good mood. The visitor is still here with her children. The youngest, about two years old is called Maria but she insists that her name is Lolita.

We all have a siesta after lunch. The light is beautiful and at about five Scharlie persuades everyone to come into the garden for a family photo. We stand around in the kitchen chatting about herbal remedies. David recommends one of her herbal teas for flatulence. He says he's been eating too much of his sourdough bread. Tomi thinks it's 'muy fuerte' and prefers her tortillas.

The tree they use for curing wounds is called Tempa. You spread sap on a fresh wound and it forms a seal. Lisote is used as an air cleaner. Albahaca or basil is used for earache. It's chopped and mixed with olive-oil which is warmed and dripped into the year. Anis, aniseed, is used for wind and a dried flower called Telo is used for insomnia.

You put it under the baby's pillow, says Tomi. Her father taught her and his mother taught him. He used to cure everyone at home, she says.

Your children seem very industrious, we say. We never pushed them but they have always worked hard at their homework, Tomi says. Maybe boys are more difficult. Luis used to live with my mother, but he stopped going to school when he was twelve and hung out with the boys, smoking marijuana and getting into trouble. He's been here five months. At first he was stand-offish. He lacked love. But now he's started to relate to Luqui.

Tomi describes how ants entered the house and ate their way into the dog-food bag. There was a line of ants twenty centimetres wide going all the way up the road, she says. You have to admire them, she says. Soldier ants are the big ones on the margins defending the workers carrying the leaves that are many times their own weight. They hand over the leaves to the smallest ants at the entrance to the nest. They're the females, says David.

After lunch Tomi takes Scharlie into the garden and shows her the various plants she uses – banana leaves for wrapping the maize tamales she makes for breakfast. She ties the leaves with string torn from yucca. They collect leaves from the plant she calls oregano though it looks nothing like English marjoram. She puts the leaves into water and boils them for a few minutes before decanting a pale green liquid which tastes pleasant.

Did you ever receive Steve's book Terra Firma? asks Scharlie. Yes I thought it was good, says David. I read it straight through. It didn't have a strong storyline, but lots of books are like that today. It has a lot of information. I liked it. My computer burnt-out just afterwards and we lost everything.

Jenny has been hoping to play Monopoly this weekend and Steve encourages her to get everything set out on the dining room table. She is such a precise self-possessed child. She asked David to be banker. We wait for Carina, Tomi and Dora to return from visiting Norma and her new baby.

As soon as Tomi and the older girls get back we start the game. Everyone plays, except Luqui who has to prepare her class, and Luis who's gone back home to get a certificate he needs.

It's a Guatemalan version of the game called Bankopoly. Jenny is determined to hold out for the local equivalents of Mayfair and Park Lane because she's won with them before. She refuses to buy anything else and watches everybody acquiring property with apparent equanimity. When Tomi lands on one she buys it from her with such alacrity that the deal causes confusion. Her animation shows what strong emotion she's hiding behind her calm exterior. We're hard put to somehow engineer for Jenny to win. Steve does it by lending her money and selling her his property with deferred payment. She goes to bed happy without a murmur when Tomi calls at nine.

Tikal

Monday   9/2/04

We are woken in the night by the dog charging into the bedroom window. Then the alarm goes off at four and Steve creeps out to put some water on to boil and wake David.

David is driving us to the airport where we are catching the plane to Tikal. The road is empty. Our man at the gate, the nice man with no teeth who David persuaded his neighbours to pay, runs out to open up. We cross railway lines on to a wide smooth avenue.

Recently an American company put in new tracks. The old ones were rusting away and there were shacks down the middle of the avenue where the tracks are now, says David.

The line runs from coast to coast, from the Atlantic to Pacific, and David hopes that it will take some of the homicidal truck drivers off the road.

He's getting a lot more relaxed about talking about his life as a secret agent. It helps explain all the oddities in his behaviour in Venezuela when he used to become vague and disappear for months at a time.

Whenever you say anything wounding to David he screws up his eyes and hunches his shoulders and makes a defensive gesture with his hands. This vulnerability had to have been his greatest asset as a spy. That and the ability to think on his feet. How could a spy reveal this depth of feeling?

We're at the airport soon after five. We check in and David joins us for coffee and doughnuts.

Without preamble Steve asks, are you Richard Owen?

Yes, says David.

Who's that? asks Scharlie.

A famous author with a couple of thrillers under his belt, Steve says. He had found the books in David's bookcase.

David smiles diffidently and says, One is about the Autana called 'The Eye of the Gods'.

I tried to retire in 1979, says David. You're not supposed to. In theory you can give three months' notice, but in practice you're supposed to stay on. I was recalled to London. I told them I had just divorced, I was broken hearted. I wanted to write a book, to buy a boat and sail round the world.

They said buy a boat, we'll lend you the money. Write your book, but quick, and get yourself off to Jamaica and find out what the Commies and Michael Manley are up to. So I wrote the book and sailed over. I wanted to write a book about the boat, all the nuts-and-bolts, ropes and tackle. But I never did.

But you wrote the thrillers

Yes. Costa Verde is about Vasquez who pulled off the biggest swindle ever. I talked about the boat book with my editor. He said keep going with the thrillers and one day I'd get a best seller.

I got in to see the boss of Reader's Digest through a contact with his wife. It turned out that an editor there had recommended 'Into the Lost World' as a condensed book. Said it was pacey. But he left it on his desk when he went on leave without putting it into the system. Sorry, we can't resurrect it now, they said.

And Lew Grade paid for an option on 'Eye of the Gods' for a film but there been some problem about filming the dinosaurs. Funny, quirks of fate that make all the difference between success and failure.

It's getting light as we go through security. It's a small roomy Tikal Airlines jet. Someone's mobile phone is playing a tune in a row in front, but he's asleep and doesn't answer. He must have had garlic for breakfast; our eyes are watering.

The flight takes half-an-hour. We have a good view out of the window, then cloud sets in and gets thicker until, as we come in to land, it's raining and Flores is in cloud. The glimpses we get are almost like England, until we see a lake, dirt roads and a gridiron town of low rise bungalows and tin shacks. We wonder if it will continue raining. Neither of us has brought a rain coat; we just have the clothes we're wearing.

We find our tour guide without difficulty

Boarding flight to Tikal

and have time for breakfast in the airport cafe before we board the minibus. It's excellent – huevos revueltos (scrambled eggs), with frijoles and platano, the fried banana we've got used to.

The minibus arrives and our guide, a slightly tubby man with luxuriant wavy black hair and a thick moustache, introduces himself.

My name is Juan. I am your guide. This is my first tour ... pause ... of the day. Ha, ha. I speak Spanglish.

He tells us he's not going into detail but we can ask whatever questions we want. That way we will not get bored with each other.

We check into our hotel – the Tikal Inn. It's simple and beautiful. The design is very traditional. There is a swimming pool in a three-sided courtyard surrounded by thatched bungalows, one of which is ours. There are trees and plants everywhere, a green lawn and garden full of birdsong, with the forest crowding to the edge. One of the very few remaining mahogany trees in the park stands proud on the paved causeway to the hotel.

We stow our bags in a cupboard in the hotel and set off at once on foot. First Juan shows us a model of the whole site at the visitor centre. He says that the University of Pennsylvania started excavation here in 1956 and then Guatemalan government took over. About twenty percent of the area was excavated or restored. This work has been stopped because they found that the friable limestone had been protected by its jungle covering and that it deteriorates rapidly once exposed. Of the buildings that are open to view three-quarters of their structure is original and any restoration has been done

Our hotel in Tikal

carefully and in accordance with the archaeological measurements. Every few years the buildings have to be cleaned again to stop the jungle growing back.

His exposition is succinct and accomplished. He hasn't learnt it parrot fashion or swallowed a guide book. He seems to have absorbed the history and organised it into an intellectual whole so that he is able to select examples to illustrate a point or give an overview when needed.

The entrance to the park is marked by a simple thatched building where an entrance fee is paid. There is a huge pimento, or allspice tree growing in the clearing. Many of the shrubs and trees look familiar but they are all much larger than we're used to.

Juan says that the forest has been protected since 1956 when it was declared a national park. This is tropical rain forest with the trees fighting for light so they are very tall. It's cool and humid and the under-storey is thick with palms – the variety with leaves like open hands which are used for thatching predominate – and maidenhair fern covers the banks on either side of the path.

In 1970 the road from Guatemala City to Flores was finished, opening up the Peten. The population exploded from 25,000 to 400,000 as people poured in and grabbed a smallholding. Juan was a teenager. His father and elder brother are chicleros. When they moved to Flores he began working on the archaeological site and became a guide in 1986.

He is proud of his Mayan heritage. He talks about their complex social and scientific systems. The Maya had concrete, he explains. They cleared the jungle and made a raised platform to form a catchment for a system of tanks and

Model of the site, helpful since much is overgrown and you get disorientated

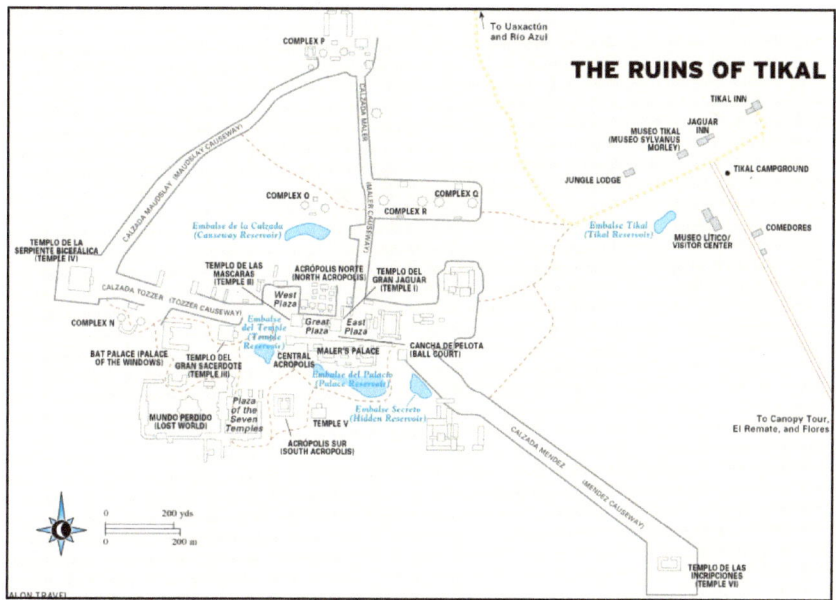

reservoirs around the edge.

The entire area of the temple complex stands on layers of crushed stone and concrete that were laid down once the jungle was cleared. After nearly two millennia of building the platform is 30 metres thick and well above the level of the surrounding jungle. At the height of its power Tikal had a population of 100,000 and occupied an area 30 kilometres in diameter. We're only going to see the central area.

The Peten is a limestone region with few natural lakes and rivers. Drains and gullies were incorporated into the platform to channel rainfall to reservoirs lined with plaster. One of these is now a picturesque pool and a home for crocodiles. Juan says they prefer eating foreign imports. Right on the edge of the pool we see a flock of toucans.

The rain has stopped as we set off into the forest. The trees tower above us, some probably over 100 ft tall. It is wet underfoot. The tracks are surfaced in limestone. Perhaps not as smooth as they would have been when the city was occupied, this means that although the path isn't muddy, it does have a shiny slick and in places it's treacherously slippy.

Scharlie constantly points out trees she knows from childhood. We stop to look at a Ceiba tree. The trees around it have been cleared to show off its

magnificent trunk and buttressed roots. It's the Guatemalan national tree and is planted in market squares in every town and city. In the forest environment they grow tall and are covered with epithytes. In Jamaica it's called the silk cotton tree and is the source of kapok.

The forest is aloud with the sounds of birds and monkeys. Where the path narrows and the trees join overhead we see spider monkeys swinging high up in the canopy. They're easy to spot with their long tails and raucous screams. Juan warns us that they often pee and crap on tourists. Howler monkeys live here too but are seen more rarely.

Juan tells us cautionary tales of people wandering off into the forest and getting lost. I finger the compass and whistle in my pocket. In spite of having a compass, says Juan, as reading my mind.

He tells us about a Canadian visitor who stepped off the path to photograph an animal and followed it a short way. He couldn't find the path but knew to walk east. He was on his way to Honduras when he was found nine days later. He survived on breadfruit nuts. Juan points out the tree and shows us how to peel the small green fruit just in case. It's called ramon. It's ground like maize to make flour for tortillas and is supposed be very nutritious. Looking across the forest it is easy to imagine getting lost.

Juan points out a Sapote, the chicle tree.

My father and elder brother were chicleros, says Juan. They were employed by Wrigley spearmint to tap chicle trees for gum. Chicle is a Mayan word.

The tree is criss-crossed with cuts in the bark. It hasn't been tapped for fifty years, says Juan. The men used to go out in gangs of thirty and built an encampment deep in the jungle. From there they went out on their own for six days at a time. They went in June and July because the rain helps the sap run.

The trees are forty or fifty metres to the crown. The men climbed with spikes on their boots and a rope round the tree. With a machete they slashed two criss-crossing channels to collect the sap into a container strapped to the base of the tree. The men got 200 Quetzales for a 200lb bag of chicle which took two days to collect. Now they get 450 Quetzales but it can take four days to tap the same amount because the trees don't yield as much.

Sometimes there was an accident. The gum collector would slash through his own rope and fall. He might be on his own miles from his camp and unable to walk. If they were badly injured, as many were after falling 40 metres, they might not be found for a week or more and were eaten. Until twenty years ago there were many jaguar, puma and panther.

Now Wrigley's get most of the gum from plantations. So there isn't the demand. But three villages still specialise in tapping forest trees. Thank God my father and brother survived, says Juan.

Scharlie asked about mahogany.

There are less and less, says Juan. The seeds are a favourite with many animals and birds.

Somehow one suspects logging may have more to do with the scarcity than birds and animals.

The chicle tree bears the naiseberry that Scharlie likes and remembers from her Jamaican childhood. The fruit is called Chico here. We had some at

Juan, our guide, telling us about chicle

David's and Tomi told us about the tree. Juan says you give the fruit to mothers-in-law because it gums up their mouths.

We pass stelae, round-topped standing stones with inscriptions, and reach a pyramid. After centuries the tree roots have pushed off the facing blocks which, piled round the base, protected the structure.

We reach the Grand Plaza, the largest cleared area.

It's not clear why this civilisation collapsed but there appears to have been a prolonged drought. Juan leaves us to wander around and Scharlie and I climb to the top of the North Acropolis where for eight hundred years Mayan rulers and aristos were buried. Then in 700AD Heavenly Standard Bearer built the two great temples on either side of the plaza.

We sit on the stone steps and watch a black vulture sail over the Jaguar Temple, Heavenly Standard Bearer's tomb. Through a small aperture in the wall we get a glimpse of the Temple of Masks where his wife, Twelve Mackaws, is buried. The Jaguar Temple is named after a carving on the door lintel. The lintel is in a museum in Basle. Juan says the Swiss explorer who found it didn't get to see it there because he died on the way home – the Mayan revenge.

Mayan society was hierarchical, Juan says. A commoner could never marry into the aristocracy so the leading families suffered from inbreeding. It was

Stellae

Our first view of a pyramid

Jaguar Temple 1, Grand Plaza, Tikal

a ruler's responsibility to propitiate the gods and predict events through astronomy. The long drought destroyed the people's faith in their rulers and they abandoned the city.

Juan says it's nonsense to think of the cities as lost because the Maya always knew where they were and continued to use them for religious ceremonies. Once the temples were plastered and coloured red but there is only the faintest trace of colour now. A carving of the rain god at least 10 ft square retains its power as he grimaces at us from beneath a protective awning of thatch.

Juan describes the costumes worn by the Mayan rulers – tail feathers of the quetzal bird which stream behind as it flies, undulating like a snake. Hence the name Plumed Serpent. The ruler would also have worn pounds of jade ornaments making his walk ungainly and powerful.

Juan takes pleasure in describing the blood sacrifice of prisoners who were given a drug which immobilised them but allowed them to feel pain. It was important to feel pain, he says. First their throats would be cut slowly with a flint knife, then their chest sliced open and, while alive, their still beating heart ripped out and shown to the populace.

The rulers did not escape pain either. They had to self-sacrifice by bloodletting. A particularly gruesome image exists of Heavenly Standard Bearer piercing his penis and his wife, Twelve Mackaws, forcing a thorn through her tongue. The fresh blood would be sprinkled over their son and heir to confer power.

Ocelloted turkeys *Coti-mundi*

The wildlife is ever present. Because animals are protected they have become used to people. A coti-mundi, its brown silky tail like a flag, scuffles around, his long nose to the ground and his bright eyes darting about. There is a squeal and a tourist has lost his lunch as the coti-mundi makes off with the paper bag. A park attendant shooes it away but too many people want to take photographs. A flock of ocelloted turkeys gobble their way across the grass, iridescent blue and gold. Brown jays squawk around the buildings while parrots, with a more distinctive screech, stick to the treetops.

We continue to Temple IV. Juan points out parrots and a roosting crested turkey. The lower parts of the building are still covered in soil and trees and there are ladders 200 ft to the top.

Juan rests at the bottom whilst we climb the steep wooden steps, almost as steep as ladders. We are puffing by the time we reach the platform. Above us rears a three-storey stone house with a roof comb soaring even higher. The view is stupendous. To the East we look towards the Great Plaza and can see temples poking out of a green ocean of forest. We walk around the platform. On all sides the jungle sweeps away to the horizon.

When we descend and Juan says we earned our lunch tickets.

Lunch is a leisurely affair, getting to know the other people in our group. It turns out that five of them are from the same Scot's family. Colin, the son, is about 20 and has been working for six months in a home for Guatemalan children with Aids. He's used his weekends to travel around. He persuaded his parents, his sister and her boy-friend to join him for two weeks holiday.

Temple IV *Climbing Temple IV*

Juan has said that if six of us book for an 'early bird' tour leaving at 6am he will stay overnight. We have to pay in advance so he knows we're serious. Scharlie badly wants go so she's organising the others into booking. She persuades four others to sign-up in advance otherwise Juan would not come back that early.

It's three by the time we finish lunch and we spend the rest of the day having showers, writing and reading and taking a muddy walk around the crocodile pool in the rain.

At supper we are joined by Chad and his partner. We talk about the process of choosing a new Democratic candidate for President and the chances of his beating Bush. The economy has taken an upturn which is in Bush's favour, says Chad. Bush is also proposing to pass a law against same-sex marriage which is likely to bring out the right wingers who don't normally bother to vote.

We discuss terrorism and the fact that in England security cameras have become accepted with hardly a murmur. While we're talking Juan turns up. 'Hola, he says. He is voluble, perhaps he's had a few drinks. He tells us that if we go walking in the moonlight the jaguar will get us.

Tuesday 10/2/04

Steve dreams he hears howler monkeys in the night and it turns out to be true because we can hear them when the generator starts up at 5:15.

As we pass the huge agave cactuses at the entrance to the hotel we see a throng of Oro Pendula, weaver birds, pecking the flowers. Juan says they are early risers. They look grey in this light but we saw one yesterday with a startling orange beak and yellow fan tail. They make nests like hanging gourds from 'old man's beard'. The female constructs the nest, which hangs like a basket a metre-long. When it's half-finished the male swings on it to test its strength. If it collapses she has to start all over again.

A silver fox slinks across the car-park, a streak of metallic grey. Until eight months ago a jaguar crossed the road here most mornings at dawn. Then a speeding motorist knocked it down and killed it. It was a pregnant female The driver was a government official so nothing was done.

Juan makes a bird sound and is answered from the forest. Scharlie tries but gets no answer. They don't speak English, says Juan. It's a Tobelejo, it's supposed to be beautiful.

Just before we enter the forest Juan asks if anyone has a flashlight and begins poking around by some steps. There is a hole in the side of the steps and Juan says it's the home of a tarantula spider. He takes a small stick, spits on it and pretty soon a spider pops its head out. Steve takes a photo and the flash frightens it and it disappears. He apologises. More teasing, and Juan encourages it out of its hole again and deftly pinches it just behind its head with his thumb and forefinger. The fangs just open a wound, he says. The poison

Juan rousts out a trantual from its nest

Scharlie tickles its tummy

is held in a sack in her mouth. It causes infection around the wound and then severe stomach cramps. Juan obviously has first-hand experience of this. On the farms, if they bite a horse, the horse loses a hoof.

He tells us that until he was 13 he lived in the jungle and his only toys were the animals. The tarantula was his favourite. He had been bitten many times. With the stick he showed us the long brown fangs. She likes to be tickled, he says. He rubs its legs and encourages people to feel how velvety it is. Scharlie tries. When you touch its stomach with the tip of your finger it's soft like our cat, Chelo's, tummy. Winnie, mother of the Scot's family, gingerly reaches out a finger and touches the spider. She's thrilled because she's frightened of spiders.

I used to tame them, Juan says. Once I made a glove for each fang. I tied a string to one leg and put it on my shoulder when I went to a friend's party. He got a shock when I embraced him.

They build the finest webs and are even able to catch hummingbirds, Juan says. We saw a huge spider when we were in Venezuela. It was about eight inches across. The Indians called it a bird-eating spider. This one is about three inches.

The jungle trail is dim, it's still not yet light. Someone whispers, jaguar! Juan grabs his binoculars. A large animal is silhouetted high on a Temple buttress. Juan is excited. It is just getting light, mist drifts between the trees and the ruins look mysterious.

No it's a weasel, says Juan.

It has a pointed nose and long bushy tail.

British weasels are small, Steve says, describing the size with his hands.

This is a Mayan weasel, says Juan. A perro lijero or Sanjol.

We watch it climb the near-vertical wall of the temple. It disappears head first into a hole, its thick brown tail waving like a flag. He's after honey.

He has a smaller relative called a Kinkaju which is also called Honey Bear, says Juan.

A little further on we hear bird-song.

That's a wren, Juan says.

How big are your wrens? asks Steve.

We see two woodpeckers with scarlet heads and white-fronted parrots. Along the way Juan gives us another tip for jungle survival. Shoots of the pacaya palm are tender and nutritious, he says. He peels of the out leaves and passes peices round. It's rather like tiny asparagus. They are delicious cooked in omelettes, he says. They were an important part of the Mayan diet.

when rubbed on the skin the leaves of another palm protect from mosquitoes. Juan breaks of a leaf and shows us how to crush it and rub the oil on. He says his father and brothers used these leaves everyday.

We ask the name of a spiny palm.

The Escoba, because it makes good brushes, also 'give and take' because it draws blood, says Juan.

It is also the only palm which has silvery white backs to the leaves and chicle collectors use it to mark a trail through the forest.

Another tree has a bronze red bark with curly slivers hanging loose. It's called the tourist tree because it goes red and peels, says Juan.

We come to a larger area in a clearing covered with Wandering Jew. Juan says it's used to make a tea which is good for the kidneys.

We reach Temple IV which we climbed yesterday, and climb it again. This time Juan comes with us. Cesare, the guide the tourists praised in the hotel visitors' book, is there already and greets Juan with 'the early bird catches the worm, buddy' jibe. They must be rivals. Later, on our way back, as we cross the Great Plaza, Cesare is high up on the North Acropolis, hands on hips, scanning the area for tourists like a black vulture. I figure he must have fallen out with the hotel. I bet the guides don't see much of the 80 Quetzales we each pay.

From the top of Temple IV, at 212 ft the highest temple in Tikal

I wonder if he makes more freelance. Winnie stays behind. She has vertigo. Cesare keeps her company.

There is no real sunrise and it's misty but the light has gradually strengthened so the forest is clear.

Juan tells us how the Mayan kept track of time. The temples are aligned to catch the sun at the solstice. On 21st June the sun enters the room behind us as the sun rises.

The Mayan divide time as follws: each year is at Tun. 20 years are a Kantun. 20 Kantun or 400 years make a Baktun. There are 13 Baktun in one period of creation which last 5200 years .

The first creation was made of wood, the second of clay, the third of flesh, says Juan. Each creation ends in catastrophe. The last age of flesh ended in a flood, like in the Bible, says Juan.

The current 4th age of maize is due to end on 21st December 2012, says Juan.

How will it end? Steve asks.

I don't know, says Juan. But I don't believe in evolution. I'm not descended from a monkey, I was made in the image of God.

We can see the tops of temples poking through the mist. There is a harsh call and a bat falcon flies over the Mundo Perdido, the palace complex we're going to next.

Juan learnt about the medicinal properties of plants from his mother. She was pure Mayan, an Ixta Mayan, the people who were here when the Spanish arrived. He says this knowledge is being lost because it's associated witchcraft.

On the top of Temple IV, – Juan telling us about the end of the creation of maize in 2012

But to make the medicine work you need that power too. It isn't sufficient to know the properties of these plants, to be effective they must be administered with the appropriate ceremony. How otherwise would one be able to tap into the energy of the other world, Juan says. The plant on its own might or might not work. To be more certain of a cure one needs knowledge of a plants place in the system of being.

I lived in the forest until I was 13 when I came out to see the world, he says. The world being Flores. He has never left Guatemala but he says he intends to visit other countries soon. His command of languages is astonishing. He says his family is surprised by his talent. He tells them it's because he was wanted. My mother was delighted by my conception. You lot were accidents, he tells them.

He is one of 14 children but only has two of his own. He says his daughter has his genes and is interested in everything but his son takes after his mother.

Juan knows his subject inside out – anthropology, history, flora, fauna, bird-life, you name it. He speaks good English and passable German to someone we meet.

What else do you speak, asks Scharlie.

My Italian and French are better than my Spanglish, he says. He is self-taught, from listening and studied for three years to get his licence as a guide.

As well as knowing the botanical names of the plants and trees Scharlie asks about, he also knows the local name in Guatemala, Mexico and Honduras. He knows what the tree was used for by the Maya and what products are exploited now. He knows what fruit it produces and in what season. He knows how the bark is used to produce a dye and what animals and birds eat the fruit or make nests from its leaves.

We enter the East Plaza as it begins to drizzle. Shame my Lady is growing at the base of a pyramid like a lawn. Scharlie loves this plant. The leaves close up when you touch them. It's called the Dormilona, the sleep plant. If your child cries in the night and won't sleep, you pick the flowers and put them under the pillow.

The pyramid here was used as an observatory. Unlike temples, which have only one staircase, this pyramid has steps on all four sides. Juan points out the horizontal panels which he says were a Teoticuahan influence from Mexico. A flock of green parakeets flies over. Then someone spots a red-headed woodpecker. Further along we see a pair of white fronted parrots. We are getting our money's worth. Many of the ruins are unrestored and some of the mounds are still covered with earth and vegetation. Unless you knew, you'd never guess there was a temple under this layer of green.

Chad asks Juan if he suffered in the Eighties.

I was kidnapped three times, once by the guerrillas and twice by the army. One time I thought I was about to die. An officer held a gun to my head and asked me to tell him about the rebels I was helping. I said I didn't know any rebels. He could shoot me, but he would be shooting an innocent man. Then the guard changed and the new officer was better.

The end of our tour is Temple V. It has been completely excavated and half the main flight of steps are renovated but they're chained off because it's too slippery and steep. It makes Scharlie feel dizzy to imagine a priest ascending these steps. At the side there are ladders we can climb which lead to an airy ledge at the top. There is little fuss about health and safety here. People have to have their wits about them.

It's time to go. Juan has another party to take round this morning after he has had a quick breakfast. We're sad to part and take his email address.

We are tired when we get back to the hotel, starving for usual breakfast. Later, after a shower, we go over to the bookshop in the museum. You can browse but the books are covered in cellophane. The shopkeeper offers to unwrap a book that has obviously caught our attention. It costs all the money we have so we say we haven't enough. She says we can pay by Visa and there is no charge. Still reluctant, she offers a discount. It's impossible to refuse. So we buy a heavyweight anthropology text and some salads servers.

In the museum there are photographs of the site when it was first discovered by Maudslay. They show the whole of the Great Plaza clear of forest and the vegetation on the pyramids chopped right-back. Yet the panels say Maudsley only stayed on site for seven days at a time. A team of chicleros like Juan's father must have been employed to do the clearing.

We pack and then sit outside writing and reading. It's sunny. We're sitting by the pool sipping banana liquados, milk-shakes.

A tall American with long hair wanders over and announces he is the messiah of Joelism.

What's Joelism, we ask.

It's my philosophy of life. I've written seven books detailing my thoughts and my travels.

Temple V *Scharlie descending Temple IV*

What's the philosophy about?

People ask me if they should go to college, and I say, did Bob Dylan go to university? Jack Kerouac is the great, great grandson of Shakespeare. Man's evolving, we're getting better, we're improving.

We look bemused.

Most of my philosophy is based on song lyrics. I write poetry all the time. The lyrics of the great pop composers like the Stones, Dylan and Van Morrison – they're like the romantic poet's Shelley and Keats.

What about your travels? we ask.

I've a book on Machu Pichu and one on the Himalayas.

Are you trying to find yourself on these travels? No I'm happy where I am, in my own skin. I've found myself. I don't carry a camera, not on the outside anyway.

Where do you come from? he asks us. Cambridge, we say. I'd like to teach at Cambridge. Words of wisdom culled from my travels, from getting in touch with my inner being. It just flows out of me. The Rolling Stones are the best thing to come out of England. The Fab Four came from Liverpool. Why there? If you're making love with the right woman who'd you rather have on CD, Ronald Reagan or Paul McCartney?

Neither! But we realise we're not expected to answer.

I'm not here in Guatemala to get laid, stoned or drunk – just produce a literary masterpiece. What's more important to human development – art or politics?

We wait for him to tell us.

I can answer my own question. Art, of course. I have dreams in which I converse with the President. The dream changes when the President changes.

Do you carry a gun? he asks.

No, we say.

I believe in peace, love, and violence when appropriate.

He sees we have a book about Tikal.

I've got a case full of books about Tikal, he says.

I lie on my bed and meditate. I write with automatic writing. I work from one to seven each day. I write on lined paper and I put the sheets in loose-leaf binders You know the files with spring clips. We call them loose-leaf binders in the States. You know?

Yes, we assure him.

And I write with a cheap Biro. I get these in packs for $10. I can get a line of coke of $10 and that only lasts an hour and these last a month. I use the blue to write and red to correct.

He gets two blue and two red ones out of his pocket. I brought extra in case I lost one on the plane, he explains.

My editor suggested down here. On the coast I can live on $5 a day. I work part-time in the post office as a mail clerk. I've run up $25,000 on credit cards writing my books and getting the first one published.

Do you have any water? he asks.

Here, says Scharlie handing him our bottle of water.

Shall I get a glass? No keep it, she says. He seems delighted.

We say goodbye and he moves away and sits with the Scot's family.

The minibus leaves promptly and we're full to capacity. Everything seems so well organised and quietly efficient. Not at all what we were expecting. We have tea in the crowded cafe in the airport. The foursome on the adjoining table light-up. They hold their cigarettes as if they're beginners. We retreat to the main concourse. Smoking we realise has not been a problem. Very few people seem to smoke – neither tourists nor Guatemalans.

El Pacaya Volcano

Wednesday 11/2/04
Back at David's we decide to climb the volcano today and are getting ready to go. Tomi decided last night that today was the day although David had been saying there was still plenty of time. We're packing our bags and making coffee and sandwiches. David is excited but doesn't know if he'll make it to the top. This is his twelfth ascent. Tomi says it's years since they've been out walking.

Scharlie feels a little squirming nervousness in the pit of her stomach. Another volcano erupted a couple of days ago and yesterday there seemed to be an extra large plume of smoke from Pacaya. The guide book recommends checking with your local met office but we don't think we're doing any of that. We're also dispensing with the guided party accompanied by armed guards that the guide book recommends. When we were discussing it David gently said he was used to taking a gun. But Tomi has made him leave it behind. She's afraid that if there is a gun fight someone is likely to get hurt.

The weather looks good and we can see the volcano with its plume of gassy steam. All the people we've talked to recently say it's been windy and cold up there and they have worn fleeces and anoraks. Tomi tells Scharlie to take a white scarf to wrap round her nose and mouth when we get near the crater because of the sulphur fumes.

The main road to the volcano is paved until we are within a mile of San Francisco de Pacaya at the entrance to the park. As we near the village boys try to wave us down. They are probably offering to be guides. David ignores them and we reach a place in the village where we can park the car. The first thin dogs we've seen rush up wagging their tails, hoping for picnics snacks. Two puppies amble up but they look unwell and have little energy.

We've met several people who have been to Pacaya and had been told by their guide that it was too dangerous to go to the crater. David says all sorts of old ladies go in high heels, so no wonder. The weather is perfect – clear skies and a light breeze.

We start walking. David says it's about three hours to the top and it's now 10:15. We all have sticks, serviceable broom handles he's issued us with. The track is cemented for a couple of hundred yards then becomes a dirt path between hedges.

A sign at the unfinished visitor centre describes Pacaya as a Strombolian volcano. This means, says the notice, that its eruptions are frequent and fairly mild. Vesuvius in contrast, is a Plinian type of volcano which is silent for centuries and then blows its top.

The path now runs in a deep rut. On either side there are steep small fields. They are cultivated with sugar cane and peaches, but we can't see any other crops, but of course it's the dry season. Soon there is forest with a sign saying take care of the plants and animals. Three women pass us carrying huge bundles of firewood. They have the loads on their heads. They are young and wearing lipstick.

After about 20 minutes we hear a horse trotting behind us and the rider shouts taxi! He has an open friendly face animated by hope.

Quiere un taxi? he calls.

David has been saying that he regrets not having taken the horse to save his energy for the loose scree. We encourage him to accept the lift. The man moves forward with alacrity and a big smile. David decides to take him up on his offer and climbs aboard. He has a good seat but Tomi says he hasn't ridden before.

We walk together for a while, but David and the horse go faster and leave us behind. Two men come out of a side path eating packets of crisps and carrying mattocks. They look as though they've been working. They seem to be eyeing us up and Tomi looks uneasy and quickens her pace.

We soon catch David who has stopped at the Mirador del Lago. The man

David atop his 'taxi'

Our first view of Pacaya

leading David's horse asks him if Tomi is his daughter. David says no, she's my wife and we have two daughters. The man looks admiring and says, she's a lot of woman.

We reach a picnic spot. There are police here, as they had been at the other rest places lower down. They are clearly making sure tourists are safe.

A big party passes us going down. The guide looks very happy and says that it is wonderful today. His name badge says his name is Eusebio. He asked Tomi if she is our guide – she looks very professional in her blue jeans and hat.

No, I'm the capitana, she says, laughing.

He tells us to go slowly, poco a poco, bit by bit, and then we'll make it.

Don't worry, says Tomi laughing, I've had them in training all week.

The vegetation thins and we reached a pastoral area of closely cropped grass where the path peters out. David has had to go another route around a stile we've climbed over. There are three more guards who ask us if we are the only ones in our party. They seem to be keeping a strict check on the people on the mountain and are in radio contact with the police who counted us in at the entrance. Soon after this the grass ends and we are on to black lava.

David rejoins us having enjoyed his ride. I hope this isn't a milestone for me, he says. I just took the horse to experience the ride.

We can see the volcano's cone now. It looks steep and no wonder it's intimidating to none mountaineers. We can see a couple of people high up on the mountain and scaling from them it doesn't seem that big, less than a thousand feet to the top.

We ascend a firm lava path to a monument on top of a knoll. The volcano

Rest at the monument before the summit cone

towers above us. Below us there is a ravine filled with tortured lava shapes and static black rivers. We rest a moment at the concrete plinth. Below us we can see the huge black river of solidified lava from the last eruption. This is where David and his friend got to when the volcano erupted.

The lava was red hot and flowing down the ravine, David says. The volcano had been erupting for days and we'd gone up to see the lava flow. We realised the volcano was not in good humour and had regretfully decided to retreat when it started to erupt. We ran for it and had just reached the flat area near the monument when the top of the mountain blew off. The molten lava lands with a splat like a cowpat, he says.

Fortunately for them there was a gale force wind which blew the debris away. At home Tomi and the girls were waiting. The girls were crying. Esta muerto, Papi! They were covered in ash and arrived home black. Only their eyes and teeth showed in the dark, says Tomi.

The path curves round to the ridge. The serious part of the climb starts now. We begin the ascent, going steadily. We take it slowly. This is the most efficient way to move. The granular rock slips under your feet and if you take quick large strides you slip backwards. By carefully placing one's feet one can conserve energy.

We ascend a firm lava path

Just below the summit cone

Enveloped in sulphurous gas from the active crater

Slowly we mount the zigzag path, the lava becoming more colourful as we ascend. Any nice coloured stones we see we pile up by the side of the track for when we descend. Scharlie wants to take back rocks for the grandchildren.

Quite soon Tomi says we are nearly there. It has taken half-an-hour. We're planning to do the 10 minute walk to the summit then descend and traverse round to the crater. David is going well. He has to stop a couple of times to reduce his heart-rate but mainly he climbs steadily. We reach a flat terrace where David says most people stop. There is steam emerging from under the rocks and a strong smell of sulphur.

We start up the final steep bit to the top. The wind changes and we are enveloped in gas. Tomi says she's not going on and David says he doesn't know if we'll make it. Scharlie looks uncertain. Steve takes off his t-shirt and puts it over his mouth. It makes an ideal mask being damp with sweat. Scharlie wraps her scarf round her face and David uses his shirt flap and starts off. We stumble upwards through the thick gas. We get to the summit and manage to take a photograph. We can't see very much.

The rocks are hot under our feet. Many are yellow with sulphur, but there are also reds and purples. We grab a handful for the grandchildren and put them into the outside pocket of Scharlie's rucksack. They're boiling hot.

We descend a little and traverse round to see into the crater. The wind has changed and is blowing the sulphurous gas away from us. We have to hurry. It is wonderfully clear as we arrive and we have a view into the bright yellow cauldron. We stand on the edge looking down into the swirling white depths.

You wouldn't want to fall down there, says Steve.

The wind shifts and we are asphyxiated again. We hang around hoping it will clear again so we can take a photo. All the time we're choking. Then the gas gets too thick to see anything and we have to give up and descend.

Back on the flat terrace away from the fumes we find some slabs and stop for a picnic – sandwiches, tortillas, coconut sweet and chocolate, sent from Canada by David's son Vivien.

Tomi, David and Scharlie lie down to rest and Steve sits leaning on one-arm. The slabs of rock are warm and we feel drowsy with the heat and our exertions. Steve has just fallen asleep when Scharlie exclaims that the sun has broken through. The break in the cloud is only momentary and a few minutes later we stir ourselves and begin the descent.

As we start down the steep path Scharlie finds a small steak knife on the scree and asks if anyone wants a knife.

David looks up and says it's his.

How did it get there, we ask.

I had it tucked it into my sock. Tomi told me she didn't want me to bring the gun.

It's a wicked looking knife, says Scharlie.

It's been sharpened both sides, says David.

Tomi laughs and brings out a little bag of cayenne pepper to throw into attacker's eyes.

Steve says you're a right murderous pair.

Further down we stop and fill our rucksack full of the rocks we've stashed.

Picnic on rocks warmed by the volcano

It's very lumpy but quite light. We get back to the monument and take-off of our boots to get rid of the small stones that have collected in the long glissade down the ash slope.

Back down at the pastoral picnic area we talk to the guards. They ask where we come from and are most impressed that David is married to a Guatemalan. They're here all day, it must be boring. They say there are 15 of them and there haven't been any incidents for four years. They have to start about seven and are here until the last group descends, which is maybe five or six o'clock in the afternoon. If someone has permission to camp, the police have a chilly night.

It's an easy walk down taking about an hour. David talks about coming back with Jenny and renting horses again for the ascent. We meet the next guided party on the way up but the top has clouded over and we don't know if they'll see anything.

Back at the car there is a troupe of little boys. One of them has shining blonde hair and European features. A German has been here, says Tomi with her throaty giggle. The leader of the group is taller and albino. He keeps his eyes almost closed and looks through his thick lashes. He says they've been guarding the car. I come prepared for this, says David. He gets into the car and starts the engine then rolls down the window and distributes one Quetzal pieces.

We trundle off. It has been a successful expedition We pass coffee plantations. Scharlie asked about the larger trees shading the coffee and if they ever use macadamia trees. We heard about macadamia from Chad, the young American on the Tikal trip.

David tells us about a gringo he knew who'd been a fireman in San Francisco but had been invalided out with a small pension and had come down here. He has a missionary zeal to convince the coffee growers to plant macadamia, says David. He gives talks and plays the fool with his poor Spanish. People didn't know what to make of him, but when the market for coffee crashed growers decided he must have something. He now has a finca and his wife makes beauty preparations from the nut oil which she sells from a shop in Antigua. We realise that David is talking about the same America Chad told us about.

We get back. The gate-man comes out cheerful as ever. The water is still off but we manage to wash in a basin of cold water. We have tea and chat and then eat a stew prepared by Dora. Another early night. A yellow moon is setting over the lake and in the calm waters a perfect reflection like a round pumpkin – a golden egg in a silver nest.

Amatitlan

Thursday 12/2/04
Today the lake is still and calm. It's cool with the merest of breezes. The mountains on the far side are shrouded in mist and the outlines of the two promontories are blurred so that it is difficult to distinguish tree-line from reflection. The world looks provisional – fresh and invigorating. It feels like a day in spring and fills us with energy.

Leaf cutter ants have made a track across the lawn. It's two or three inches wide and nine or ten yards long. They were going for a tree they fancy in the corner of the garden. David says the track wasn't there at 7:30 this morning when he was out so they've done it in an hour. He's poured poison down the hole but the ants build their entrances with a siphon so the poison only discourages them and doesn't get anywhere near the queen or the brood chambers.

There's a whole city under there, says David pointing to the lawn.

We discuss what we might do today. Tomi and David have so many jobs to do to keep the whole show on the road. The water is still off and nothing is resolved.

I suppose the committee is still trying to get people to pay up, says David.

Steve remembers that in Venezuela simple things could get so complicated. It's partly poverty – many of the people may find it difficult to raise the money. Its partly corruption – they paid before and someone's stolen the money. And it's partly character – for many people honour and pride are more important than anything and this traps them into ways of thinking and acting.

David filling his water tank

It would probably work better if the women were in charge, says Scharlie. The sort of drive that Madre Innes has to build her Church and the practical resourcefulness Tomi shows in running her household is what's needed.

David orders a tanker of water. The truck will bring 2,000 litres for 200 Quetzales. The tank in the garden only holds 1000 litres, so the rest will irrigate the lawn. Tomi is worried that the tank is dirty so Scharlie offers to get in and clean it. Steve says he'll take photos. Tomi holds him to his word and asks him to go out with the camera. David climbs in with his socks on in case it's slippery. He's using a light to see what he's doing. It's Steve's job to make sure the light doesn't fall into the water and electrocute him.

Later, Steve has just dropped off to sleep when he's woken by the sound of gushing water and realises that the tanker must have arrived. He goes out to take more photographs. This water business is turning into a real saga.

Scharlie is reading David's book 'Costa Verde'. Tomi goes out to the supermarket to get supplies, but forgets coffee, so David and Steve have a reason to go out. At the mall they talk about writing. It turns out that David and his editor, Dennis Fawcett, had a business deal to write jointly.

We were aiming for the American suburban market, says David. Lots of action, fast pace and a light touch with the sex scenes. I lost interest after the second one. I'd have liked to have written the book about sailing.

The best writing was the first of the two expedition books, he says. I worked with Jessica, a US reporter. It only took ten days. I'd hammer it out on the typewriter, correct it in ink and hand it over. She produced the clean version. She even posted it off for me. After a few weeks of not hearing anything I rang and was told, don't be a dummy, it's fine, that's why you didn't hear.

I'm not interested in the recognition

Reading David's novel - 'Costa Verde'

or the Booker Prize, he says. I wrote fore the money. It's a matter of finding the right formula. Plus you have to be in your thirties, with a good few years of production in front of you and you have to be able to churn them out at a rate of one a year.

We really tried with the Morgan thrillers. I was on telly, on a quiz show. And I did radio interviews. Fawcett arranged for a few of his friends to ring and ask where they could buy it, who it was published by and how much did it cost type questions. But we didn't break into the big time.

What percentage of aspiring authors do? Steve asks.

One per cent of one percent, says David.

We have a big lunch and have just settled down on the veranda when Jenny asks if we can go to the golf club for a swim. We feel sorry she doesn't get enough play, so show enthusiasm and suggest we walk.

We ask Tomi if that would be alright and she thinks we mean will it be safe.

No, we try to explain, would it be socially acceptable arriving on foot when all the other members come in expensive cars.

Tomi says it will be fine, but when Dora hears we are walking she raises her eyebrows.

The club is so close and the walk so pleasant it seems crazy to take the car and go round the long way. David is keen, so we walk.

The pool is empty and we have the place to ourselves. We all swim. It is delightful watching Jenny playing sharks with her father. On the walk back she finds small slivers of obsidian in the dust of the footpath.

The doorman at the nunnery has blocked the road with stones. Apparently the school bus has knocked over the fence Madre Innes put up across the entrance to the dirt road down to Amatitlan. David is furious because this is the only place the bus can turn and if the driver is hassled he won't come and collect Jenny. David decides to move the rocks and starts tossing them out of the way.

The doorman watches stolidly. David tells him that this is a public road, it's not part of the monastery and they have no right to block the road.

As we walk back he says, I don't know how people do it, people with full-time jobs. Tomi and I spend our whole time just running the house.

David's thinking about getting back to writing but he says he would need more time without distraction.

He's good at writing, says Tomi fondly.

Two people have already been today about the water. Some neighbours want to buy water from Madre Innes and others don't. David says he's not getting involved unless everyone agrees. There is only one set of tubes so if someone doesn't agree it won't work.

Steve is reading David's novel. He is up to the bit about Morgan trying to get alongside the swindler's niece.

That was always the worst bit – trying to dream up ways of making contact, says David. Wracking your brains to think of a way in. Going through all the moves before making a call to avoid making a mistake. And having to play the fool at times to allay people's suspicions.

Friday 13/2/04
Steve finishes David's novel while Tomi and David take Scharlie to find the tree that cures wounds. Scharlie comes back with a bit of branch and the news that the next-door neighbour, has done a deal with Madre Innes for the nuns' water supply. He's arranged for a new plastic pipe from the nun's supply straight to his house. David is upset that the neighbour hadn't discussed it.

Steve gets out Charles Brewer's book on Sarisarinama. David says he hasn't looked at it. There is an introduction by Charles and lots of photographs but the main text is from David's book 'Into the Lost World'. David is upset that Charles used his book without his name on the cover.

Charles admitted he wanted the glory, says David. He's xenophobic about foreigners claiming anything to do with Venezuela.

Swimming at the golf club

He's probably just as possessive and selfish with anyone, including Venezuelans, says Steve. In his book Charles says his passion for exploration grew out of his childhood interest in minerals. Charles is a vociferous advocats of environmental protection and campaigns for the Amazon region to be closed to visitors. Yet when we were in Caracas in 1990 Ramon told us Charle's company had been mining with hydraulic pumps, the most damaging of mining techniques.

Are you Welsh? Scharlie asks. David's pseudonym is Richard Owen and his hero, Morgan, is from North Wales.

I'm one-eighth English, says David.

Is Anna Gwyneth Nott, the person your book is dedicated to, your mum?

Yes.

And your dad? asks Steve.

Parry Jones. Nott was my stepfather. I'm illegitimate.

That's something else we have in common, Steve says.

My mother was in the workhouse in Walton when she had me, says David.

You can't top that, says Scharlie.

There was just a line on my birth certificate in the box marked father, says David. The registrar must have done it with a ruler and the pen must have jumped off the line where it hit his thumb.

Tomi collects Jenny from school and we go to the thermal spa in Amatitlan. There are two pools – one with cold-water, one with hot. The pools are surrounded by gardens and we have a panoramic view of the lake. It's one of Tomi's favourite places. Next-door there is a house with a large gallery and below the house, in the immaculately kept garden, there are two wooden chalets. Many of the trees and shrubs are in bloom.

We been coming here for 15 years and have never seen anyone, says David, other than the gardener who lives in that small lean-to.

Tomi says she has always admired this property and that they would have liked to have bought one of the houses if they could have found out who owned them.

The elite families who own these lakeside properties clearly like to hang on to them. We're not sure we'd like to live so close to the lake front with its eateries and loud music.

Tonight we are going to Antigua for a meal and a night on the town. Tomi drives so David can talk. She's a quiet, careful driver. It's a while since they've have been out and she's excited.

Was it difficult maintaining your cover as a journalist?

Yes, I had to disappear whenever a big story broke and the press pack turned up, says David.

Didn't the Firm square things with an editor like they do in the spy thrillers?

No newspaper could be caught covering me, they'd lose all credibility. No I was on my own; I didn't even have a telephone number to ring and no one to ask for help. They drill it into you. If you're exposed, they'll disown you.

I always thought your job as a journalist looked pretty thin, says Steve.

Once or twice at best I was a stringer for the Telegraph. I did pieces for them and for the Economist. But I couldn't pretend to be correspondent for either of them. My sister Ann twigged. Correspondent for the Telegraph! I haven't seen much of your stuff in the newspaper recently, she said.

Once I had to go down to the Dominican Republic. We were met by a press officer. There were gendarmes standing round. I had to read his list upside down, trying to see who might be missing. One of the Telegraph reporters hadn't turned up so I pretended to be him.

Did you get to know some of the correspondents?

Didn't know any of them. Philby was up to the same tricks in Beirut posing as a reporter for the Economist. Once they rang the High Commission to check on me. They rang the Telegraph who said they'd never heard of anyone called Nott. I had to bluff my way out.

So why were you a spy, why did you do it? asks Steve

At first it was flattering, an adventure.

David and Jenny

But why go on?

No-one to turn to and no one to bother you; no colleagues; no set hours. You could decide where to go and who to see; when you've had enough and when to pull-out. I liked that.

I can see that the independence was attractive, but what was the motive? Why were you doing it?

David seemed to stiffen and said, because I didn't like communism. We were at war, just like the Second World War. Hitler's plan was for the Gestapo to take over a couple of Cambridge colleges. Imagine that. And the Russians would have been no better. Just think of the Stasi in Liverpool.

So you were a cold war warrior?

Well whatever I was it finished with the end of the Cold War.

You must have done a good job.

Sure the whole thing collapsed didn't it.

We sit quietly and reflect on what David has said as Tomi drives down the curving black road into Antigua.

It's the best road in the country, says David. Dual-carriageway, no potholes, cats eyes both sides and in the middle. It would do justice to Germany.

What I discount in comparing myself with David is the generation gap, thinks Steve. He's 15 or 17 years older than I am. He was a teenager during the war, I was born at the end. For me the war is history – vivid history, brought alive by my father's stories, but history none-the-less. For David the war is part of his life. Fighting Hitler and fighting Communism was real and immediate.

We think the conversation is over. We're not sure how Tomi is reacting to all the seriousness, after all this is supposed to be a night-out. Then David breaks the silence.

Richard Sorge was one of the best. He was a German working for the Russians in Japan. He used to get so drunk he regularly crashed his bike. They caught him in the end, That's why we know about him. He had a radio and managed to get a message to Stalin that the Japanese wouldn't invade Russia. So Stalin was able to move two million men from the East. Two million! That turned the war. I don't know what they did to him but I bet it wasn't pretty.

I imagine you were good at deception, says Scharlie.

David turns and grins. Good at dissimulating you mean. Sneaky, crafty. Someone once said that the reason I got away with it was because I had a face like a priest. Mashed up, but no-one would believe that anyone with a face like mine could be up to what I was.

You look quizzical as though you can't quite believe what people are telling you. I guess people want to convince you, to confess, says Steve.

There is a passage in David's book. 'When he had first come to Costa Verde it was because it seemed to offer an opportunity for unlimited licence … the tropics were the best place to get away with whatever you wanted.'

I really admire the way you and Tomi have made a family for so many people, says Scharlie.

It's nothing. It's so easy, says David, with the deprecating smile and the habitual twitch of his nose.

David's done pretty well, whispers Scharlie as we reach Antigua. Seventy-five and with a lovely wife and happy family.

Did well to survive at all, says Steve.

It's our treat to take them to dinner. We stop near the plaza and a man appears offering to look after the car. The Doña Isabel, where we go first, only does snacks so we walk round the block looking for another restaurant. Finally we decide. Tomi wants to get it right.

She begins with an old favourite from Jamaica – avocado cut up in chunks in bean soup. David and Tomi choose to share a mixed grill called 'Bill Clinton'. It's also called 'un poco de todo' or a little of everything. In the entrance lobby there are photographs of Bill with the owners.

It's a leisurely meal since we don't have to get to the Casbah until after ten. David matter-of-factly declines alcohol. Don't take that first drink, he says. He starts to share Scharlie's ice cream but stops when he realises it is laced with rum.

David says Millie and Tomi came here on their own and had partied until four or five in the morning. They stayed over in a hotel and got back about ten in the morning, then took the girls back the following evening.

We go back to the car for Tomi's wrap and the man appears like a shadow. But he has to wait because we set off walking again.

We cruise around until David says there it is. The Casbah is just beginning to fill up when we arrive. A sign says no admittance without a cedula or passport. But David dives in, saying, they'll probably relax it. Bouncers in black T-shirts frisk us and look in Tomi's handbag. Then we're on the dance floor giving a good impression of a salsa.

The dance floor is overlooked by a gallery full of people. The majority watching are Guatemalan; the majority dancing are tourists. The atmosphere is friendly and there is no sense of tension, let alone danger. Just lots of young people out to enjoy themselves.

There are more blond-haired folk here than one sees in the streets, but also a lot of locals down from Guatemala City. Young men stand on tables at the side doing complicated arm and hand movements and scanning the girls dancing. One seems completely self-absorbed looking down at his feet, his hips moving to the salsa beat.

The music is not overpowering and the disco lighting gives the impression we are moving well. Tomi with her make-up looks stunning and completely relaxed as she dances with David. He's about three times older than most of the people here but is quite undaunted. He keeps the rhythm with neat economic movements and has the stamina to keep going a couple of hours. We dance until one and don't feel as tied as we expected. The young man is still watching the car when we get back and David gives him ten Quetzales.

The ride back home is smooth and gentle. We play music and keep getting Abba until Steve discovers how to wind back the tape. Straight into bed and then Luqui comes in saying she won't see us in the morning because she has to get up early and wants to say goodbye. She throws her arms round us and gives us a kiss on the cheek. We're touched.

Saturday 14/2/04
Today we leave. It seems too soon. We've settled in and have got used to the new rhythms and surroundings. Last night we complimented Tomi for the way she runs the household.

Yes, she says, it's very peaceful here.

David has been worried about taking care of the family financially. He would still like to write a best-seller. We try saying that he has given his children things more valuable than money, but when faced by his bluff embarrassment we find we can't phrase our feelings clearly. It's about values and putting in your time, as David would say. It's about the importance of education. But more than this it's about caring for others, and putting people before oneself. Ironic that David defines this as the crucial thing wrong with Latin America.

Breakfast is calaloo soup, a kind of spinach that Scharlie likes, followed by pancakes.

A que hora sale al aereopuerto? What time do you leave for the airport? Jenny asks in a bold voice. David screws up his eyes thinking and Jenny says, Y el karate?

She's been talking about going to a new class at school that starts this morning. This causes David a momentary panic working out how to fit everything in.

David and Steve take her to school. A little boy opens the gate they go round to where they find the class. It's outside and there is a teacher and three boys.

David hangs back at the corner and says very gently, What do you think Jenny?

She looks for a moment.

Do you want to try?

Si, yes, says Jenny, and they set off to meet the teacher.

David explains how he has to take visitors to the airport and asks if he can leave her.

Back home we finish packing. While Steve makes coffee Scharlie tries to finish David's novel. Tomi and Dora go about tidying the house and putting Luqui's and Carina's things back in our room. They have all gracefully accepted beening moved into the one room. David calls it the dormitory. Maybe they like sleeping together.

Steve is on the veranda scribbling his journal when David shows him the dedication he wants to put in his one remaining hardback copy of 'Eye of the Gods'. It reads. To Stephen Platt, a good friend and lead climber on the real ascent of the real Autana from David Nott, aka. Richard Owen 14th February 2004.

Steve doesn't know waht to say. It is such a generous gesture. He stands

Saying good-bye to Chispe (Spark)

and they embrace the Venezuelan way, hugging and slapping each other on the back.

Then it's time to go. We hug Tomi and Dora and climb aboard. At the school Jenny looks excited and full of what she's learnt in the class. She looks hot and wants to go back home and tell them about it. So we go back and Steve takes a quick snap of her with her dad in front of the bourganvillia.

She's probably in the kitchen demonstrating karate already, says David, as we drive out of the gate.

The trip to the airport goes smoothly at first and then we hit heavy traffic, so David turns round and tries another way. He says that the problem is the buses that stop anywhere. We try going on the outside of the queue, but it's hair-raising trying to squeeze back in as a truck bears down on us. We pass street markets and finish the film by snapping fruit stalls and street vendors. At least we are seeing a different slice of life.

The road is lined with single-storey shops and houses. The whole city is low rise with only a few tall buildings in the centre. Every shop that sells anything worth having either has an armed guard with a pump action shotgun or the sales staff are behind heavy grills. We wonder if we should roll up our windows.

David keeps cool. We're supposed to be at the airport at eleven, three hours before our flight. It's now nearly twelve but we tell ourselves that we still have plenty of time.

Scharlie asked about the brightly painted buses.

They're American school buses that are too dangerous to be used in the States so they send them down here,

Getting to the airport

says David.

Near Jenny's school there was a yard with dozens of buses still painted in their school-bus yellow. There were quite a few men wandering around looking them over. Maybe they have just had a new delivery from the States.

David is concentrating on driving. Steve asks him to clarify a point for his journal.

I shouldn't have been blabbing about my work, says David.

The journal's only for private consumption, Steve says.

I wish I'd kept a journal, says David. I didn't even keep a log when I was sailing.

I had an uncle who was a spy in the forties, said Scharlie. His name was Simmonds-Beecham. Did you know him?

I didn't know the names of any field agents and I only knew a handful of controllers by name. Didn't even know where head office was until they built that new building.

So it wasn't like James Bond going to see Moneypenny to get his plane tickets?

Hell no.

What's the difference between MI5 and MI6?

MI5's internal counter-espionage. I only had dealings with them once. Someone gave me a letter to take to his contact in London. The contact took me up to a Cuban safe house. MI5 couldn't believe it, they had been trying to find the safe house for ages.

What's your attitude to Cuba then?

I never went to Cuba, says David.

Did someone else cover Cuba, we ask.

I don't know, says David shrugging. He's really good at this.

What about Cuban health and education? asks Scharlie.

Well they were subsidised by the Russians. That's finished now of course.

But it's a phenomenon and so is Castro, says Scharlie.

Sure, says David. Now the island's a centre for sex tourism.

It's only a hundred yards, says David.

We think he means the airport. I can't imagine an airport right in the middle of all this urbanisation. But it turns out to be the T-junction that has been holding us up. We sail through and get on a faster section of road, behind a truck carrying water bottles. Steve jokes that all we need is for it to fall in the gulley by the side of the road. A bus pulls out of the line of oncoming traffic forcing the water truck to stop. David is furious. He winds down his window and shouts, 'pedazo de mierda', at the driver and holds up his finger in the gesture most likely to offend a Latin male. The water truck edges past slowly, the road clears and we are at the airport.

We join the check-in queue. They are opening everyone's luggage and Scharlie is worried that she will have her seeds and cuttings confiscated. But hers is the only case they don't check. We pay our airport tax and join David for a coffee.

Scharlie finally finishes the book and is enthusiastic in her praise for the exciting ending and the quality of the whole thing. She says he should write another.

An American couple are sitting next to us with a pilot.

They have money dripping off them, says David.

I don't expect they'll be sitting near us, Steve says.

The man is overweight and dressed in a blazer, slacks and baseball hat. He rubs a large coffee stain on his white tennis shirt.

We go down to the boarding gates and ask if we can buy coffee to take back with us. David looks around and sees a coffee stand. We've been looking for a shop. He sweet-talks the girls into selling him a packet of coffee they use in their own machine. We embrace again. This time we really hug each other. Maybe this will be the last time we see each other. When we were leaving Tomi had said this is your home and they are there to receive us when we return.

It's as if you entered a calm harbour at the end of a life of storms, Scharlie said earlier over coffee.

Really is that how it looks to you, said David. Some people can only see the hassle of life in the tropics.

He seems pleased that we recognise and appreciate the peace and harmony of his life.

David reading his English language newspaper